KU-458-314

Arms of the County Councils of SCOTLAND

by

David L.H. Patton

In proud memory of my uncle,
and of my cousin,

2nd/Lieut. DAVID PATTON, 2nd Bn. Scottish Rifles.
Died of wounds, Passchendaele, February, 1918

Pte. JAMES PATTON, 25th Bn. Australian Imperial Force.
Died of wounds, Rouen, January 1917.

First Printed 1977

Published by
ARGYLL REPRODUCTIONS LTD.
Port Charlotte, Isle of Islay

Printed by Highland Printers Ltd., Diriebught Road, Inverness

FOREWORD

The purpose of this book is to attempt to show the wealth of history that is waiting to be discovered in the arms of Scotland's County Councils—County Councils that ceased to exist during May 1975.

Scotland had 37 counties. Four of these were counties of Cities (Aberdeen, Dundee, Edinburgh and Glasgow), leaving 33 landward Counties, each with a County Council. These County Councils have been taken in order, and the order used is that set out in a Brieve of Precedency from the Lord Lyon King of Arms, dated 21st June, 1956; this order was based on the order at the last meeting of the Scottish Parliament in 1707.

A word on heraldry may be appropriate, albeit from an amateur. A coat of arms was originally just that, a surcoat with the heraldic device painted or sewn on; the shield was next similarly painted. Attention now-a-days is focussed on the shield rather than on the coat. The heraldic design is recorded in writing in the blazon; the blazon is definitive, though an artist can portray the blazon as he sees fit, so long as he complies with it. What the artist is not permitted to do is to make changes, be it in colours or in adding or subtracting from the blazon. When the blazon is portrayed this portrayal is known as the emblazonment.

The arms of the County Councils are all treated in the same manner; first the blazon is given and on the opposite page is given the emblazonment of the shield. Among the earliest symbols, or charges, is the Celtic winged blade in the arms of Argyll County Council. Surpassing in number the Celtic charges are those from families of Norman origin, and then again there are those charges of distinctly Scandinavian origin, the whole admixture going to make up that amalgam that is Scotland. For the sake of uniformity, only the shield of the armorial bearings is shown, and the motto given where there was one. In addition, six of the County Councils had a crest, while three Councils had supporters. A special type of coronet was designed for the use of County Councils and this is shown in the frontispiece, encircling the map of Scotland. The script used in the frontispiece is adapted from that used in the Book of Kells.

The text given below each blazon is intended to give the reason for the blazon—using heraldry as a visual-aid to bring out the history of each county. With some County Councils this explanation can be given very shortly—in these cases a brief history of the territory is given. In expanding some of the county histories, reference has been made to regiments active as recently as the Second World War. In mentioning some of our last World War regiments, it was thought only fair to mention them all, and this has been done. In giving these brief subjective county histories, two aims were in mind; firstly to give an historical story for those readers with a passing interest; and secondly to whet the appetites of those with a potentially greater interest.

With as small a nation as Scotland, it is not surprising to find many historical connections between counties. In gathering together the various histories, two points have emphasised themselves to the author. Firstly the tremendous unifying influence Edward I of England had on Scotland—hardly the influence Edward of England would have wished, virtually welding together warring Scottish factions to make a nation—and secondly, the remarkable way in which highland Scotland has influenced lowland Scotland, to the extent that throughout the world highland dress and music have become the outstanding characteristics of the Scottish nation.

History is not just a matter of looking back, but of appraising the present to see "how we got this way", and having arrived at the present, giving a stable standpoint from which to advance into the future. It is hoped this book may help to illustrate, through heraldry, some of the influences that went into the making of the Scotland of today—and that from "today", Scotland can go forward and play a constructive role in the world of tomorrow.

"Logiealmond"
Campbeltown, Argyll.

David L. H. Patton
May, 1976.

ACKNOWLEDGEMENTS

I would like to acknowledge the help so cheerfully given by Mrs Catherine Kerr, Campbeltown, in drawing the arms of the County Council of the County of Fife — so much better and more quickly than I could have done! My thanks are gladly given to Scott Cameron, Esq., in so willingly and meticulously reading the draft of this book, and for his encouragement and many suggestions. To Mrs Isobel Mitchell, Dalivaddy, Campbeltown, for her very patient typing — and re-typing! I am much indebted to Captain Graham Donald of Dunyvaig, F.S.A. (Scot.), for his guidance in Gaelic; also for the help given by the County Clerks of our late County Councils.

The reader is asked to remember that the author is an amateur, in history as in heraldry, and if the reader's appetite is whetted he should go to source to find out — there-in lies the fun! Any errors are entirely the responsibility of the author.

My thanks too, to Mr Colin Roy of "Argyll Reproductions" for his encouragement throughout, and for publishing this work with the approval of the Lord Lyon.

David L. H. Patton.

CROSS-REFERENCES

Where a cross-reference can usefully be made, the number of the appropriate County Council is given in brackets in the text. On the back cover is a map of Scotland showing the counties, each with its number.

D.L.H.P.

CONTENTS

— Order of Councils —

1. COUNTY COUNCIL OF THE COUNTY OF MIDLOTHIAN

"Or, a lion rampant Vert, armed and langued Gules, surmounted on a fess Azure charged with three suns in their splendour of the field".

The green rampant lion is a supporter from the arms of the Primrose family, the senior representative of which is now the Earl of Rosebery and Midlothian; the Primroses take their name from the village of Primrose in Fife. The blazing suns on their blue ground come originally from the arms of a knight of Norman ancestry, Sir William Kerr, son of the 1st Earl of Ancrum, and are now marshalled in the arms of the Marquis of Lothian; the heralds differentiated the arms of William, 1st Earl of Lothian from those of his father, Robert Kerr, who was subsequently — 2 years later — created Earl of Ancrum, in 1633.

Midlothian is Scotland's senior county — doubtless because it has for long contained the nation's capital, Edinburgh. Edinburgh was not always the capital of Scotland, but the matter was clinched when James IV built his Palace of Holyroodhouse beside the Abbey of Holyrood, built by David I.

Indeed, not only was Edinburgh in Midlothian, but the "Heart of Midlothian" was in Edinburgh. The site of the old Tolbooth, the "Heart of Midlothian," is marked in granite setts in the High Street near the Mercat Cross. Not far away but further down the High Street, can be seen in the road, metal plates, indicating the site of part of the Flodden Wall hastily erected after the disastrous folly of the Flodden encounter of September 1513, weeks after James IV had mustered his army on the Borough Muir of Edinburgh. Just over 200 years before, in 1303, at Roslin to the south of Edinburgh a relatively small Scottish force led by John Comyn, Lord of Badenoch, and Sir Symon Fraser of Tweedale (6) so soundly trounced an army led by Edward I of England's Scottish Secretary, that Edward had to come north yet again in his seemingly tireless efforts to attempt to subdue the Scots.

Midlothian has given birth to two regiments that stand in the Order of Battle of the British Army. The elder of the two was raised by the Marquis of Argyll, and was known as Argyll's Regiment. Argyll raised this unit originally in 1639 to serve under the Scottish Privy Council (which to a very large extent was Argyll himself) to enforce the National Covenant in the Highlands. In 1642 Charles I gave the regiment his blessing and dispatched it to Ireland — such was the initial birth of the Scots Guards (3).

The second regiment still with us associated with Midlothian was indeed at one time known as The Edinburgh Regiment, a distinction they gained while as the Earl of Leven's Regiment they showed remarkable steadiness in the face of Bonnie Dundee's highlanders at Killiecrankie in July 1689 — the year of their formation (cf. The Cameronians, under the County Councils of Lanark and Dumfries). It is interesting to note that in the name by which this unit is known today, The King's Own Scottish Borderers, the border originally involved was between lowland Scotland and highland Scotland.

One way or another the Viscount Dundee and his kinsman the Marquis of Montrose have left their mark on the British Army; and not only in the existence of regiments raised to oppose the leadership of these two Grahams. To this day the regimental canter of both The Royal Scots Dragoon Guards and The Royal Regiment of Artillery is "Bonnie Dundee", while rather ironically the marchpast of the 2nd Battalion The Cameronians (Scottish Rifles) was "The Gathering of the Grahams" (16).

MIDLOTHIAN COUNTY COUNCIL

2. COUNTY COUNCIL OF THE COUNTY OF EAST LOTHIAN

"Gules, three bars Ermine, over all a lion rampant Or, armed and langued Azure".

The "background" to these handsome arms, the red and ermine bars, comes from the arms of the Marquis of Tweedale but harks back to earlier days, and to the Giffords of Yester in East Lothian. A Gifford settled in Lothian in the reign of David I, and his son Hugh Gifford was granted the lands of Yester (from Cymric, *ystrad*, a strath) by William the Lion. Before 1409 another Hugh Gifford died without an heir, and his daughter Johanna, the heiress, married Sir William Hay of Locherwart. From this union arose the family of the Hays of Yester and Locherwart, a family which obtained the titles of Lord Yester in 1488, Earl of Tweedale in 1646, Marquis of Tweedale and Earl of Gifford in 1694 (and Baron Tweedale in the U.K. peerage in 1881). It is just possible that the lion rampant comes from the arms of this King William. As it happens the present County Buildings at Haddington are erected on the site of a palace of William the Lion's.

If William the Lion was not the originator of the East Lothian County Council's lion, one or two other contenders readily could be found within the county, starting from the one-time Earldom of Dunbar. The Earls of Dunbar were originally of Celtic stock; it is the wife of the 9th Earl, Patrick, who is best remembered. Patrick married Agnes, a daughter of Bruce's companion Thomas Randolph (29). Agnes was made of stern stuff, for she it was who held Dunbar Castle for five months against an English force in 1338, and whose name goes down in history as the dauntless "Black Agnes".

Within the county, just north of Haddington, lies the village of Athelstaneford, reputed to be the site of a battle between a joint force of Picts and Scots, and a Saxon king Athelstane. It is claimed also that in the sky during this battle there appeared the blue and white pattern of the St. Andrew's cross which became adopted as the national flag of Scotland. The St. Andrew's cross tale is lost in the mists from which perhaps it came but the name Athelstaneford is certainly curious, for it happens that *ath-ail* is Gaelic for stone-ford.

In 1625 John Hepburn, a cadet of the Hepburns of Athelstaneford, raised a company of men, which rapidly grew to a regiment, for service with Gustavus Adolphus of Sweden. This unit got royal approval from the Scots Privy Council under Charles I's authority in 1633, and was known as Sir John Hepburn's Regiment. The regiment is very much with us today, and indeed is the senior line regiment in the British Army, known now as The Royal Scots (The Royal Regiment), the 1st of Foot, with a history befitting a regiment whose founder and first Commanding Officer became a Marshall of France (11). East Lothian is a county of rich farmland, and appropriately enough the local yeomanry regiment, The Lothians and Border Horse, wore as a cap badge a wheat sheaf. The unit, with a history going back to 1797, formed two armoured regiments in the 1939-45 war.

There is one village in East Lothian which many Scotsmen have cause to know — Prestonpans — where in 1745 Prince Charles Edward Stewart's highland army surprised at dawn and quickly routed the Hanoverian army commanded by Major-General Sir John Cope. Poor Sir John Cope! Since the battle of Prestonpans in 1745 John Cope has been the indirect cause of rousing successive generations and countless numbers of Scots soldiers from their slumbers, for the cocky, stirring pipe tune "Hey, Johnnie Cope, are ye wakin' yet?" is a popular reveille among Scottish regiments.

EAST LOTHIAN COUNTY COUNCIL

3. COUNTY COUNCIL OF THE COUNTY OF BERWICK

"Argent, on a mount Vert, a bear Sable, collared and chained Or, standing in front of a tree Proper".

These are "canting" or punning arms. The tree is a Scots or wych elm, and the pun is reference to the county's name, "bear wych" or "bear wyck". In the emblazonment shown opposite, the tree has been portrayed with the characteristic profile of a wych elm (11).

In 1018 Malcolm II, King of Scots and Picts, expanded his kingdom by expelling the English from Lothian and the Merse; not for the first time King Canute could not stem the tide — and his army was defeated at Carham, on the south of the Tweed. The death of the Maid of Norway in 1290 (30), caused Scotland's aspiring magnates to meet Edward I of England at Norham in 1291. The reason? For Edward to decide who should be King of Scots! Edward readily agreed to this task, the contenders first acknowledgedging Edward I of England as their feudal superior. Edward announced his decision in November 1292; the result of the 'Great Cause' was that John Balliol was declared King, and crowned at Scone (16) on St. Andrew's Day 1292. This sorry process would not have been necessary had the Treaty of Birgham worked as planned. At Birgham, between Carham and Norham, in 1290, it was agreed that the Maid of Norway, Margaret, Queen of Scots, should marry Prince Edward of England, and that Scotland should suffer no diminution of her independence. Margaret died before reaching Scotland, and in time Prince Edward became Edward II of England, who had trouble with his van at Bannockburn, and had perhaps the most unenvied end of any English monarch, in Berkeley Castle, Gloucestershire, in 1327.

Edward I turned the screw a bit too tight even for John Balliol — or "Toom Tabard" as he was known — and a Scots raid was made into England. This was countered by Edward I with furious retaliation culminating in the Sack of Berwick in March 1294. Berwick 1296 was also the place and time of the signing of the "Ragman Rolls" after the final humiliation of John Balliol. The Balliol family had not had enough punishment, for John's son, Edward Balliol, had himself crowned at Scone in 1332, and shortly afterwards had to flee from Annan (Dumfriesshire) in unseemly haste. 1333 saw Edward Balliol back again, when, with the aid of Edward III of England, he laid siege to Berwick. A Scots army marched to raise the siege, but at Halidon Hill the English longbow took its toll and Berwick was not relieved. Edward Balliol yielded to Edward of England a considerable portion of Southern Scotland, and this was probably the best thing he did, for it started a resistance in Scotland, led by Sir Andrew Moray of Bothwell. Meanwhile, Scotland's rightful King, David II, was in France, growing up. Unfortunately the French do not seem to have taught him the right things. In 1346 David invaded England and was soundly defeated and captured at Neville's Cross, Durham. In 1357 the Treaty of Berwick was drawn up to secure the release by ransom of Scotland's precious King.

In 1461 Henry VI of England sought refuge in Scotland while passions raged south of the border over red or white roses — for this sanctuary Henry VI returned Berwick to Scotland. Berwick was again 'in the wars' in 1482. James III had trouble with his two brothers, so much so that he locked them up in separate castles, but the elder, Alexander, Duke of Albany, escaped and fled to England. In due course, Albany gathered an army and with the support of Richard, Duke of Gloucester, invaded Scotland in 1482. The Scots — yet again — were divided; James marched from Edinburgh to meet Albany, but was pursued by Archibald Douglas, 5th Earl of Angus (32). Angus 'belled the cat' at Lauder when he met up with his King — he hanged the King's unmartial favourites over Lauder Bridge. The King, Angus and Albany returned together to Edinburgh, when Albany was made G.O.C. Scotland. But while all this was going on, Richard of Gloucester seized for himself Berwick, and Berwick has remained in English hands since. The next major event in Scottish history happened just across the Tweed on a small hillock by the village of Branxton in Northumberland. The place Flodden, and the time, September 1513. If the strategy behind Flodden was doubtful, the tactics were unrealistic and irresponsible. The memory of the Scot's stand around their misguided King has not yet been erased from the nation's memory. There is pride mixed with incredulity in the nation's recollection of Flodden, a memory kept green by that haunting air commemorating the battle, "The Flowers o' the Forest".

The track across the Merse was thrang once again at the time of the none-too-enthusiastic betrothal of Mary, Queen of Scots, to Henry VIII of England's son, Prince Edward (4). As the idea cooled, the traffic on the old track grew to a roar, while Henry VIII of England conducted "the rough wooing" on his son's behalf. The ruins of Dryburgh Abbey bear testimony to Henry VIII's powers of persuasion. In 1648 Cromwell blew up Coldingham Priory, and two years later, in 1650, one of his generals, George Monck, raised a regiment in the Berwickshire village of Coldstream. Monck's Regiment in years to come was to win world renown as the Coldstream Guards.

BERWICK COUNTY COUNCIL

4. COUNTY COUNCIL OF THE COUNTY OF ROXBURGH

"*Azure, a unicorn saliant Argent, horned, maned, and unguled Or, the tail tufted of the last; on a chief of the second a hunting horn Sable, stringed and viroled Gules, between two esquires' helmets of the field*".

MOTTO: "*Ne Cede Malis Sed Contra Audentior Ito*".

The origin of the charges in this case is conjectural as the arms are old (1798). It could be that the unicorn is one of the supporters of the Scottish Royal Arms, as Roxburgh was (along with Berwick-on-Tweed, Edinburgh and Stirling) one of David I's "Four Burghs". The county of Roxburgh is in a sense unique, for though the town and the castle, once among the most important in Scotland, have all but disappeared, yet the name Roxburgh proclaims itself now as loudly as ever (23).

History maybe has a way of repeating itself; certainly there was around Roxburgh a very profound thud on the drum of time, echoed centuries later in Scottish history and both blows spelt trouble for Scotland. The first blow occurred in the 12th century when Malcolm the Maiden's brother William, Earl of Huntingdon, (later William the Lion) was campaigning in Normandy with Henry II of England. William suggested to Henry that Cumberland, Westmorland and Northumberland should be returned to Scotland. This suggestion brought forth an explosion of Plantagenet wrath, and if this alienation from the English monarch tended to point the Scots towards France, and if this was the first glimmer of the Auld Alliance, then Henry's wrath has certainly reverberated down the years. At any rate, by the Treaty of Falaise in 1174, Henry put his thumb firmly on top of William the Lion, and the major castles of Scotland — Edinburgh, Stirling, Jedburgh and Roxburgh — were garrisoned by English troops. In just under 200 years another humiliating event took place, this time inside Roxburgh Castle. Edward Balliol, son of "Toom Tabard", in January 1356 virtually sold the Kingdom of Scots to Edward III of England for a lump sum plus an annual retainer.

Roxburgh Castle figures once again in Scottish history, but the time is now appropriate to remember that Roxburgh is also the county of the great abbeys, Jedburgh, Kelso and Melrose. It is in Melrose Abbey that the heart of Robert the Bruce is thought to have been buried on being brought back from Spain (7). The great abbeys again come to the fore in history but first the castle of Roxburgh once more claims attention for in the summer of 1460, James II laid siege to Roxburgh Castle. The castle had been in English hands for over 100 years and James was determined to have it back. James II had a passion for guns and as he watched the cannon balls batter the castle walls, a type of cannon known as a bombard had a misfire, the bombard exploded and James II was killed.

Roxburghshire has four main towns, three of them with abbeys and the fourth without. But that fourth has something very special in its history of which all Scots are proud, and that town is Hawick. In 1514, the year after Flodden, an English raiding party crossed the border yet again. The party was spotted. The Border's manhood and indeed Scotland's had been decimated at Flodden, but the youths of Hawick rose to the occasion. At Hornshole Bridge the Hawick callants virtually wiped out the English raiding force — an achievement commemorated in Hawick by an equestrian statue of great vigour; in fact "statue" is not the right word for this monument, it seems to move and be alive with pride of accomplishment.

The second mighty thud on the drum of time occurred barely 30 years after the Hornshole Bridge engagement. This profound happening was also about an engagement, but this time of a different kind. When James V died at Falkland Palace in 1542, his infant daughter, Mary, became Queen of Scots. The English royal house was Protestant, the French royal house was Roman Catholic. Scotland, once again with a minor as sovereign, was in a state of flux. England was anxious that her northern neighbour be Protestant also — so anxious in fact that Henry VIII of England forced the Scottish Regent, James Hamilton, 2nd Hamilton Earl of Arran, into betrothing Mary, Queen of Scots, to Henry's son, the future Edward VI of England. When this betrothal seemed to be losing impetus, Henry tried to keep it alive by intimidation. His form of intimidation was the devastation of south-east Scotland, known wryly as "the rough wooing" and to this day the ruins of the Roxburgh abbeys stand as gaunt reminders of English diplomacy of the 16th century. And once again the effect was the same — predictably — alienation of the Scots from the English, and the strengthening of Scotland's links with France.

The Latin motto of the County Council in translation reads "Yield not to evil but rather press on more boldly". Roxburgh County Council's arms also had a crest, one of only six of the County Councils to have had this distinction.

ROXBURGH COUNTY COUNCIL

5. COUNTY COUNCIL OF THE COUNTY OF SELKIRK

"*Argent, on a mount in base, a stag lodged reguardant, in front of an oak tree, all Proper*".

MOTTO: "*Leal to the Border*".

The arms of the County Council of Selkirk depicts a stag at rest in Ettrick Forest. Though the arms were matriculated as recently as 1927, similar emblems can be traced back through Selkirk's history for nearly 200 years. The larger town in the county, Galashiels, has an unusual motto, "Soor plooms". The origin of this goes back over 600 years, and recalls the casualties suffered by a small English force during an "attempt", when they were successfully set upon by the men of Gala — the engagement taking place shortly after the English had been stealing plums, and that was in 1337! This incident sets the scene well for much of the history of Selkirkshire and the Borders, a more or less constant raiding and counter-raiding. The raiders were known as reivers, and there is a fine statue of a border reiver in Galashiels. The county town Selkirk, has also a most moving statue, but immeasurably more poignant. It depicts a battle-weary soldier just able to raise a banner, and the short inscription says everything — "O Flodden Field".

In the Selkirkshire of the time of Flodden, 1513, there lived a youth with a remarkable talent for leadership, in fact not only was he at Flodden, and a survivor, but he was knighted there — at the age of 15. This man was Sir Walter Scott of Branxholm and Buccleuch, both designations being household words in Scotland to this day. Scott of Buccleuch was utterly opposed to Archibald Douglas, 6th Earl of Angus (second son of "Bell the Cat", who had advised against Flodden, and whose eldest son, the Master of Angus, was killed there). The Earl of Angus was guardian of the infant James V, and chief protagonist of the English party in Scotland, and he waged a civil war of his own in the Borders — in the King's name. Scott of Buccleuch was a wholehearted opponent of the English, and together with Elliot of Redheugh attempted to wrest the King from the Earl of Angus in an engagement at Darnick, near Melrose (Roxburghshire), in July 1526 — this bid was not successful. When eventually James V took the reins of government into his own hands, he set out to bring some kind of order to the Scots' side of the Border and to this end Scott of Buccleuch in due course progressed to be Warden of the Middle March.

The next shattering event in the county was in a sense worse than Flodden, for it was Scot against Scot in the internecine strife following in the wake of the National Covenant — all in the name of Christianity. In mid-September 1645, less than eight months after Inverlochy, (19), Montrose, the King's G.O.C. Scotland was surprised at dawn by General David Leslie and the army of the Covenant. Montrose was an outstanding tactician and leader of men, and in his astounding career to-date he had always had by him Alasdair MacDonald — Colkitto — who commanded the sons of Somerled — the highland host. In September 1645 Alasdair and his highland light infantry were elsewhere settling old scores of their own — no doubt against the arch-covenanter — but that was quite coincidental. At Philiphaugh Montrose was without his most experienced highland shock-troops and no doubt General Leslie had been informed of this, as he had been of Montrose's position. Montrose fought a defensive action, but there was little hope . . . Montrose escaped to fight again, for at Philiphaugh the "Sword of the Lord and of Gideon" prevailed and truly there was "no quarter" and that went for the women-folk of the Royalist army as well. The Clergy of the covenant army had ample practice that day in administering the *coup de grace* and the *quietus.*

Just a little up the Yarrow Water from Philiphaugh stands the ruined 15th century Newark Castle. It was to Newark that Anne, Duchess of Buccleuch, retired after the execution of her husband the Duke of Monmouth, in 1685. Anne, Countess of Buccleuch, married James, Duke of Monmouth in 1675 and on their marriage they were created Duke and Duchess of Buccleuch. On the failure of the Monmouth Rebellion, while the Duke was executed, the titles of the Duchess in her own right were unaffected. Another executed for his part in the Monmouth Rebellion was the 9th Earl of Argyll, (11, 13), whose father had met a similar fate in 1661 for his part in Covenant policy making — just 11 years after Montrose, whom he had brought to the gibbet for opposing the Covenant. After the Restoration in 1660, Montrose's limbs, which had been distributed for exhibition throughout the kingdom, were gathered together and given a state funeral in St. Giles's, Edinburgh.

SELKIRK COUNTY COUNCIL

6. COUNTY COUNCIL OF THE COUNTY OF PEEBLES

"*Quarterly: 1st, Sable, five fraises Argent; 2nd, Azure, a horse's head couped Argent; 3rd, Vert, a golden fleece; 4th, Or, fretty Gules, a chief embattled of the last charged with two thunderbolts of the first*".

MOTTO: "*Onward Tweedale*".

The fraises or strawberry flowers, are an heraldic pun; from the Norman knight with the strawberry flower or fraise charges came the "fraisers" or Frasers. In this case the Frasers in question are the Frasers of Oliver Castle and also of Neidpath, who make their first appearance in Scottish history in the 12th century. There was a Symon Fraser of renown in Tweedale before there was a *MacShimi* in Lovat. Sir Symon Fraser of Tweedale was captured at the Battle of Methven in 1306, and then executed by Edward I of England. It was Edward of England's obsession with acquiring Scotland, and also his manner of attempting to achieve his aim, that caused searing resentment north of the border. The heat generated virtually forged the peoples of Scotland into a nation; a nation hammered and beaten into shape on the anvil of Edward's desire to dominate. Edward was well-named "Hammer of the Scots"; he would have done well to remember the law that enunciates that "for every action there is an equal and opposite reaction". The horse's head in the second quarter is from the arms of the Horsburghs, a family on record for almost as long as the Frasers, and indeed their companions in arms. The lands of Horsburgh in the county were in the hands of the family until the begining of the 20th century, and the castle of Horsburgh until 1953.

The third quarter shows the "golden fleece" and signifies the importance of sheep farming in this county. The fourth quarter is a singular honour being the arms of a long-serving Lord Lieutenant of the county who was also County Convener for a considerable time, namely Michael G. Thorburn of Glenormiston. The County Council had also the distinction of having both a crest and supporters for their arms.

Among the first names to be associated with Peebles-shire is that of Kentigern, the apostle of Tweedale. Kentigern is perhaps better known as St. Mungo, the patron saint of Glasgow, but his teachings in Tweedale are recalled in the kirk at Stobo where Kentigern carried out his early ministry. In August, 1299 Peebles was the scene of a violent quarrel between Bruce and the Red Comyn, John Balliol's nephew — a sign of things to come, culminating in the murder of John Comyn, Lord of Badenoch, by Bruce in 1306 (8). Drochil Castle to the west of the county was a stronghold of the Douglas Earls of Morton; work on extending the castle ceased on the execution of James Douglas, 4th Earl of Morton, in 1581 (12, 32). John Murray of Broughton, in the county, was secretary to Prince Charles Edward Stewart during the 1745 Rising. Murray of Broughton was subsequently captured, but freed on turning King's Evidence against Symon Fraser, Lord Lovat (19).

In Dawyck Woods, near Stobo, horsechestnut trees were early introduced into Scotland in 1650, and larch in 1725. Peebles-shire has also strong ties with R. L. Stevenson, Samuel Crockett, Mungo Park, John Buchan and his sister O. Douglas.

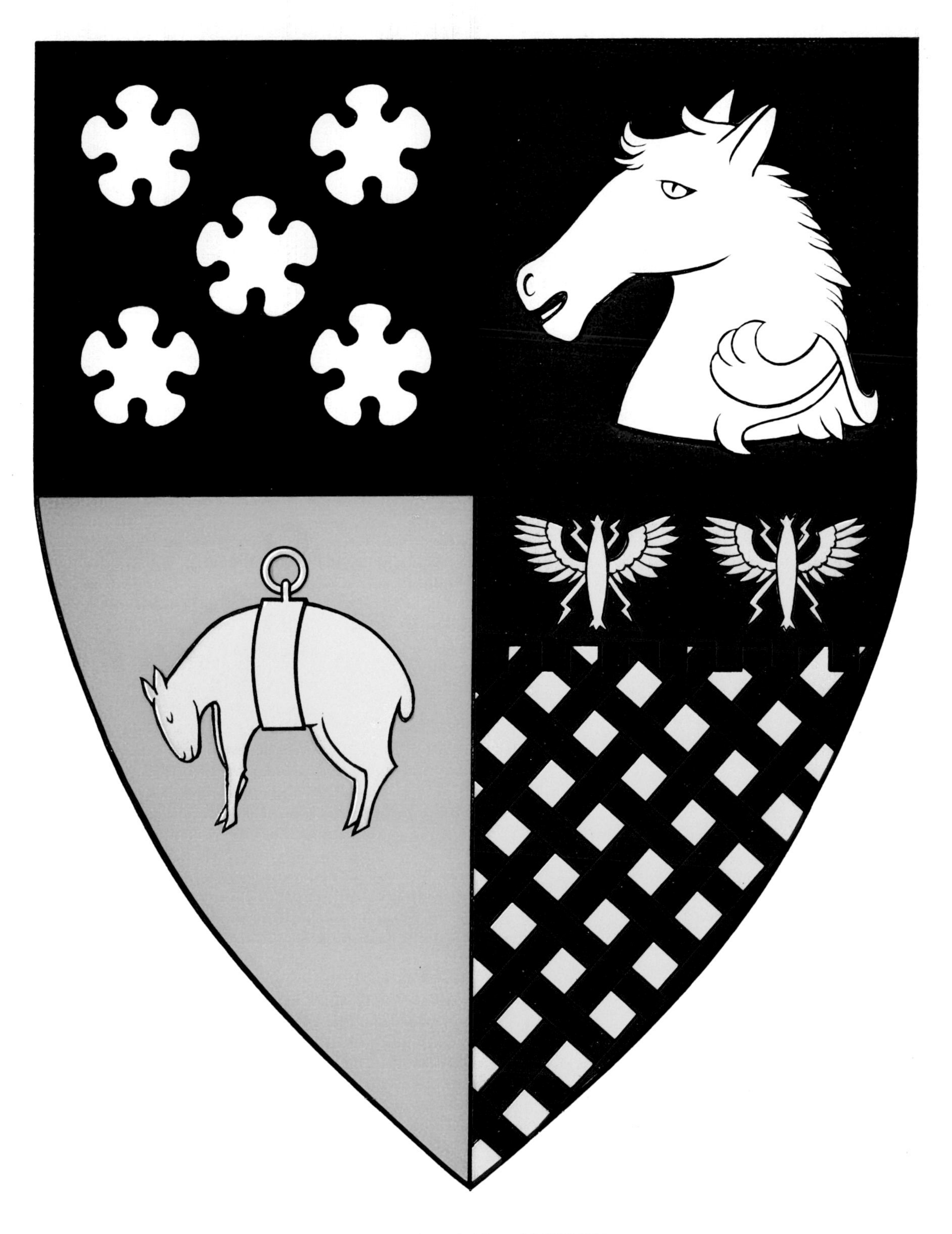

PEEBLES COUNTY COUNCIL

7. COUNTY COUNCIL OF THE COUNTY OF LANARK

"*Parted per chevron Gules and Argent, two cinquefoils pierced in chief, and a man's heart in base counter-changed*".

MOTTO: "*Vigilantia*".

Perhaps the most effective of our County Councils' arms, because of their bold simplicity, although the arms of the Hamiltons and the Douglases have seldom lain so peaceably together, as witness the "cleansing of the causeway" in April 1520. The Latin motto meaning "Watchful" is derived from the motto of the Aitchesons of Rochsolloch and Airdrie, which is "*Vigilantibus*".

The cinquefoils are from the arms of the Hamiltons, one of the most prominent families in the county. At one time a Hamilton was high on the line of succession to the Scottish throne, James Hamilton, 2nd Hamilton Earl of Arran becoming heir presumptive on the death of John Stewart, Duke of Albany in 1536. In the arms of the Hamilton families the cinquefoils are ermine (12).

The heart is from the arms of one of the most renowned families in Scotland — the Douglases. The most famous of the name, the Good Sir James (the Black Douglas) did not marshall the heart on his arms, though it was he who earned the augmentation. It was Bruce's last wish that his heart be taken to the Holy Land for burial. This mission was entrusted to the Good Sir James Douglas, who with a party of knights set sail for the Holy Land and Jerusalem. On their way however, they tarried in Spain to help fight the Moors. In battle Douglas advanced too far into the fray, was cut off, and hurled the casket containing Bruce's heart ahead, meaning to follow or die — the Good Sir James died in that mêlée in 1330. The heart of Bruce was brought back to Scotland for burial in Melrose Abbey (4). The first record of Bruce's heart on the Douglas arms is on the seal of William, Lord of Douglas, c. 1332, eldest son of the Good Sir James. This William was killed at Halidon Hill (3) in 1333 along with his uncle the Regent, Sir Archibald Douglas. The brother of the William killed at Halidon Hill was Archibald, known as "the Grim", 3rd Earl of Douglas, and Lord of Galloway (26).

Scotland's urge for independence had its first irrevocable impact in Lanark itself where in May 1297 Sir William Wallace killed the English Sheriff of Clydesdale — this act ignited the tinder-dry heather of Scotland's discontent, and the fight was on (13).

Think of Lanarkshire, and one thinks of The Cameronians. The Cameronians were ardent followers of a Covenant preacher, Richard Cameron, who was killed by a party of dragoons — possibly John Graham of Claverhouse's — in 1680. Cameron's followers had a very militant faith and in 1689 they formed themselves into a guard for the meeting of the Convention in Edinburgh. James, Earl of Angus, only son of the 2nd Marquis of Douglas by his first wife, offered to form these disciples of Richard Cameron into a regiment in support of the Protestant William of Orange. This offer was readily accepted and at the village of Douglas, on 14th May, 1689 the Earl of Angus's Regiment was formed (8). The name of the regiment soon changed to The Cameronians, and this name stood by itself until 1881, when the regiment was "paired" with The Perthshire Volunteers (Light Infantry) (16) and the combined unit was styled The Cameronians (Scottish Rifles). The Cameronian's first action was in the year of their formation, when they stemmed the highland tide at Dunkeld, immediately after John Graham's posthumous victory at Killiecrankie (1).

Lanarkshire was also the birthplace of two territorial cavalry units which took part in the 2nd World War, as gunner regiments. The Lanarkshire Yeomanry was raised in 1819 as The Upper Ward Yeomanry; The Queen's Own Royal Glasgow Yeomanry was raised in 1848 as The Glasgow and Lower Ward of Lanarkshire Yeomanry — Glasgow was then part of Lanarkshire, but since became a county in its own right. The cap-badge of The Lanarkshire Yeomanry was based on the double displayed eagle charge of the royal burgh of Lanark; in the 1939-45 war the unit served as 155th and 156th Field Regiments, Royal Artillery. The Queen's Own Royal Glasgow Yeomanry — cap-badge the sovereign's Scottish crest set between thistles — served as the 54th and 64th Anti-Tank Regiments, Royal Artillery.

LANARK COUNTY COUNCIL

8. COUNTY COUNCIL OF THE COUNTY OF DUMFRIES

"*Argent, a saltire Sable, in chief a man's heart Gules imperially crowned Or, on a chief of the third, two mullets of the first*".

The basic design — a saltire and chief — is common to several families of the county. Here the black saltire on a silver field recalls the arms of the Maxwells, Earls of Nithsdale, and the Johnstone Marquises of Annandale. The red chief with its two silver five-pointed stars is a feature of the arms of some of the cadet branches of the House of Douglas.

The royal burgh of Dumfries has many moments of historic note, the most dramatic undoubtedly being the impulsive murder of the Red Comyn in the church of the Grey Friars in February 1306 by Robert the Bruce. This put Bruce in a well-nigh impossible position from which he took the bold way out. He gathered his followers and made for Scone, where he was crowned King of Scots the following month (16). It is the heart of Bruce that was later emblazoned on the arms of the Douglases. The imperially crowned heart is first found in the arms of William Douglas, Lord of Nithsdale (died c. 1392) and was first added to the arms of the head of the House of Douglas by the 11th Earl of Angus when he was created Marquis of Douglas in 1633.

A mullet, or five-pointed star, of the Douglases forms the central feature of the cap-badge of The Cameronians. The regiment's 1st Battalion was raised in 1689 at Douglas in Lanarkshire, and the first Colonel was the Earl of Angus, son of the Marquis of Douglas. The regiment was disbanded in 1968 but lives on in the Army Cadet Force Units in Lanarkshire and in the Combined Cadet Force of Kelvinside Academy, Glasgow. For more about this regiment, see under the County Councils of Lanark and Perth.

In the village of Tinwald was born William Paterson, who at the age of 36 founded the Bank of England in 1694. William Paterson's was also the mastermind behind the Darien Scheme. In 1695 he had established the "Company of Scotland for trading with Africa and the Indies". This venture, prompted by the English Navigation Acts which barred Scottish ships from trading with the English colonies, was to have half its capital subscribed in England, but was fatally frustrated by the East India Company's withdrawing the security for English capital to ensure its own monopoly. Paterson decided that Scotland should have a colony of her own, and the Isthmus of Panama was selected — a disease ridden area as the builders of the canal found out for themselves in later years. The scheme was virtually fated before it got under way. Three expeditions in all were sent out between 1698 and 1699, but, ill-equipped in a hostile and unhealthy land, the project was disastrous in financial terms as well as in manpower. The Darien Scheme proved a crippling blow to an already none-too-wealthy nation. William III, King of England and of Scots, was perhaps playing a waiting game, for he offered no help whatsoever, and the colonists were expelled by the Spaniards in 1700. Just three years later the Scots passed the Act of Security as a preliminary step towards union with England. This union took place, for better or for worse, in 1707.

In Dumfries itself, Devorgilla's Bridge spans the river Nith to Maxwelltown, so commemorating that outstanding Galloway character (26).

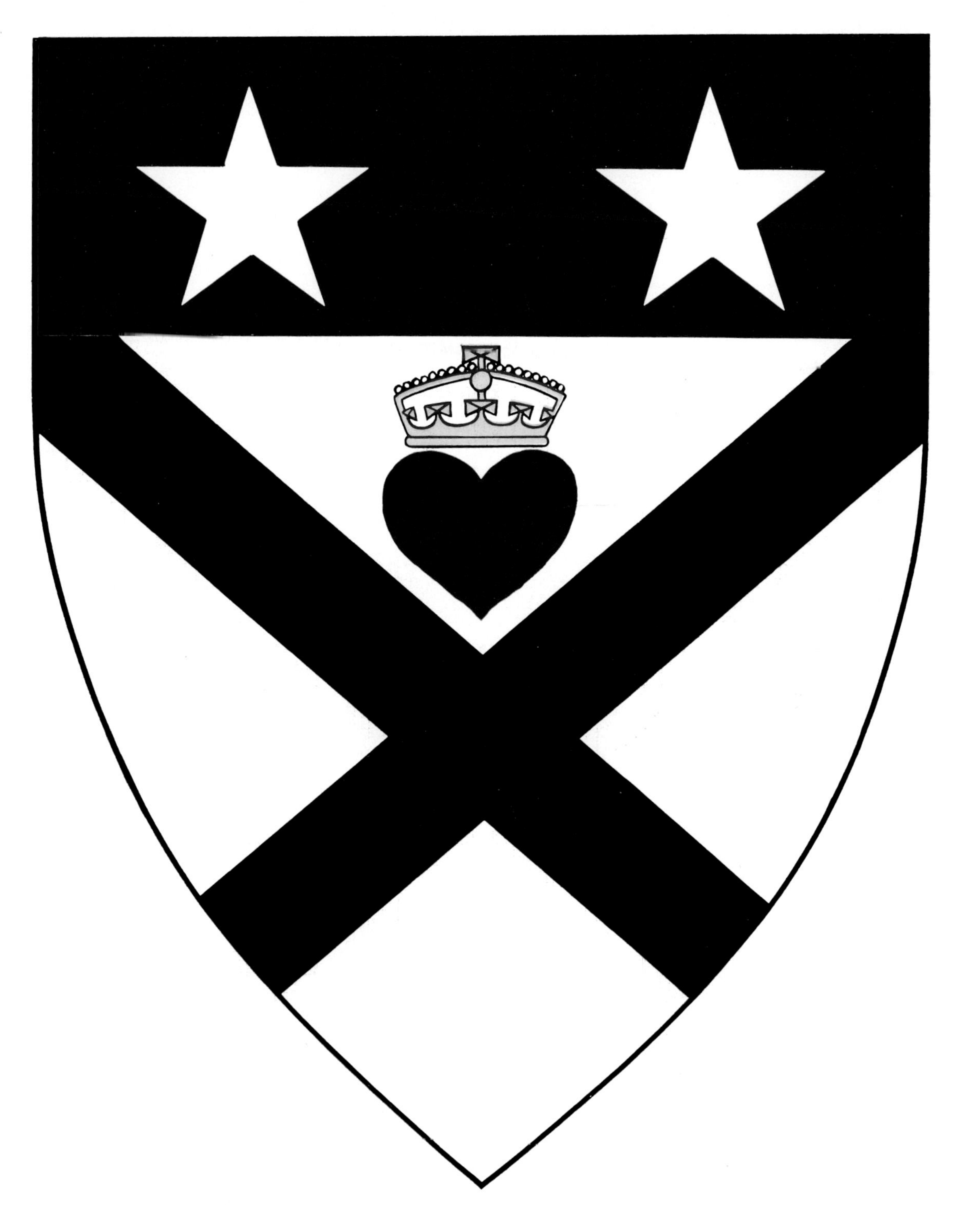

DUMFRIES COUNTY COUNCIL

9. COUNTY COUNCIL OF THE COUNTY OF WIGTOWN

"Per pale indented: dexter, Azure, a lion rampant Argent, armed and langued Gules, crowned of an antique crown Or, and gorged of an antique crown Vert; sinister, Gules, a chevron Argent, and issuing from the sinister chief a quadrant of the sun arrayed Or; on a chief Azure, having a fillet Ermine, a saltire Or, charged with nine lozenges also Azure".

The arms of the County Council of Wigtown are not only very striking, but like those of our other counties, steeped in history. This Council's arms are made up from three families with ties with Wigtownshire. The explanation for the fillet of ermine is that each of the families attained the peerage, albeit one family found it too hot to hold on to.

Starting at the top are the arms of the Dalrymples with the colours reversed. The Dalrymples were bonnet lairds in Ayrshire; around 1450 William of Dalrymple married a relation, Agnes Kennedy, who was heiress of the lands of Stair on the river Ayr. A descendant of this union, Sir James Dalrymple, as Lord Stair, was created a Lord of Session under Cromwell, and by chance President of the Court of Session after the Restoration of the Royalty. Bishop Burnet gives us a contemporary word-picture of this man, who married the heiress of the small Wigtownshire estate of Carscreugh. The son of this marriage was to win notoriety as the Master of Stair, Sir John Dalrymple, Secretary for Scotland, who was the architect of the Massacre of Glencoe (1692). This massacre was but the tip of a plan, whereby, to quote the Master of Stair, "I think the clan Donell must be rooted out, and Lochiel . . . "

On the left (the herald's dexter) is the Lion of Galloway, differenced by a green antique crown as symbolic of a County Council. The MacDowalls were the ancient Celtic Lords of Galloway, and more is mentioned of their silver lion under the heading "County Council of the Stewartry of Kirkcudbright" (10).

The silver chevron on the red ground is from the arms of the Fleming Earls of Wigtown. The sun shining through in this division is from the seal of Wigtown Town Council. The Flemings rose at the expense of the Comyns, and were granted by Bruce the forfeited Comyn lands in the Lennox (11). Sir Malcolm Fleming of Cumbernauld became Earl of Wigtown about the end of the 13th century, after the removal of the Comyn Earls of Buchan as Sheriffs of Wigtownshire. It was Alexander Comyn, Earl of Buchan, first Sheriff of Wigtownshire, who built Wigtown Castle; this Alexander Comyn was also a grandson of Alan, last of the original Celtic Lords of Galloway (i.e. he was a nephew of Devorgilla of Galloway). Malcolm Fleming was followed as 2nd Earl of Wigtown by his son Thomas. The Flemings could not cope with their Celtic landholders and the situation got snarled up — so Earl Thomas offered to sell the land and the title of the Earldom of Wigtown to his neighbour, who was very good at coping — Archibald the Grim, 3rd Earl of Douglas and Lord of Galloway. The offer was accepted in February 1372 — the price £500—the King approved and the land of Wigtown passed to the Douglases, though not the title, which lapsed.

WIGTOWN COUNTY COUNCIL

10. COUNTY COUNCIL OF THE COUNTY OF AYR

"*Quarterly; 1st, Gules, issuant from the sea in base undy Azure and Argent, a castle triple-towered of the last, masoned Sable, windows and port of the first, the towers capped by pointed turrets Vert, each having a ball Or; 2nd, Argent, a chevron Gules; 3rd, Argent, a shakefork Sable; 4th, Or, a fess chequy Azure and Argent*".

MOTTO: "*God Schaw the Richt*".

Here history is told simply but boldly. The castle is that of the royal burgh of Ayr — that the castle is a royal castle is readily seen by the door and windows being emblazoned red — the castle was built in 1202 by William the Lion; nothing of this castle now remains. The red chevron on the silver field are the arms of the Celtic Earldom of Carrick, an off-shoot of the Celtic Lordship of Galloway, created by William the Lion, to curb the power of the Lords of Galloway. The first Earl of Carrick was Neil MacDowall, grandson of Fergus of Galloway. Robert the Bruce's mother was Marjorie, heiress of Neil, the last Celtic Earl of Carrick. Robert I himself was Lord of Annandale and Earl of Carrick — as was his father — before he became King of Scots. The black Y on its silver ground is for the family and district of Cunninghame, while the fess chequy of the Stewarts is for the district of Kyle. Smack in the middle of Kyle is Ochiltree. Andrew Stewart, 2nd Lord Ochiltree, was a grandson of James Hamilton 1st Hamilton Earl of Arran. Andrew Stewart's second son was James Stewart, Earl of Arran, succeeding to the Earldom on the death of the 3rd Hamilton Earl (12). The Stewart connection with Kyle, however, goes back much further. Walter the 1st High Steward possessed Kyle, and for a time the district was known as Walter's Kyle, and later Kyle Stewart.

The motto is interesting, being taken from the gravestone in Kilbirnie Kirkyard of Captain Thomas Craufurd of Jordanhill, renowned for his capture of Dumbarton Castle in 1571 from Mary, Queen of Scots. Captain Craufurd was born in Place Castle, Kilbirnie, was captured at the battle of Pinkie, Midlothian, and then spent some years at the French Court. He was the sixth son of Laurence Craufurd, of Ayrshire stock, who held the lands of Drumry in the Lennox where now stands Drumchapel. Thomas Craufurd was born in 1530, the year his father built the Peel Tower of Drumry close by the Peel Glen. Besides capturing Dumbarton Castle, Thomas Craufurd has other claims to fame. While in France he served in the French king's Scots Guard, and on the death of Henry II of France Thomas came home and found himself laird of Jordanhill. After the capture of Dumbarton Castle Captain Craufurd was involved in planning and conducting the siege of Edinburgh Castle in 1573, and as part of his reward he received lands in Partick, adjoining Jordanhill. In 1577 he was elected Provost of Glasgow and was responsible for building the first bridge over the river Kelvin — a bridge that lasted over 300 years.

The burgh of Ayr must be remembered for "the black parliament of Ayr" held at the Barns of Ayr on the outskirts of the town c. 1296, when so many of the early leading followers of Sir William Wallace were hanged — and very quickly avenged (13).

For long Ayrshire has been associated with The Royal Scots Fusiliers, raised in 1678 by the Erskine Earl of Mar to oppose the Covenanters. As the "Earl o' Mar's Greybreeks" the regiment successfully opposed the Covenanters at Bothwell Brig in 1679, but were not so fortunate at Killiecrankie in 1689. In January 1959 the "Fusilier Jocks" were amalgamated with The Highland Light Infantry (City of Glasgow Regiment), to form The Royal Highland Fusiliers. Another unit intimately associated with the county is The Ayrshire Yeomanry (Earl of Carrick's Own), raised by Lord Archibald Kennedy in 1793. During the 2nd World War this unit formed the 151st and 152nd Field Regiments, Royal Artillery. The cap-badge of The Ayrshire Yeomanry — the head of a lion between the wings of an eagle — is claimed to be the crest worn by Robert the Bruce, as Earl of Carrick.

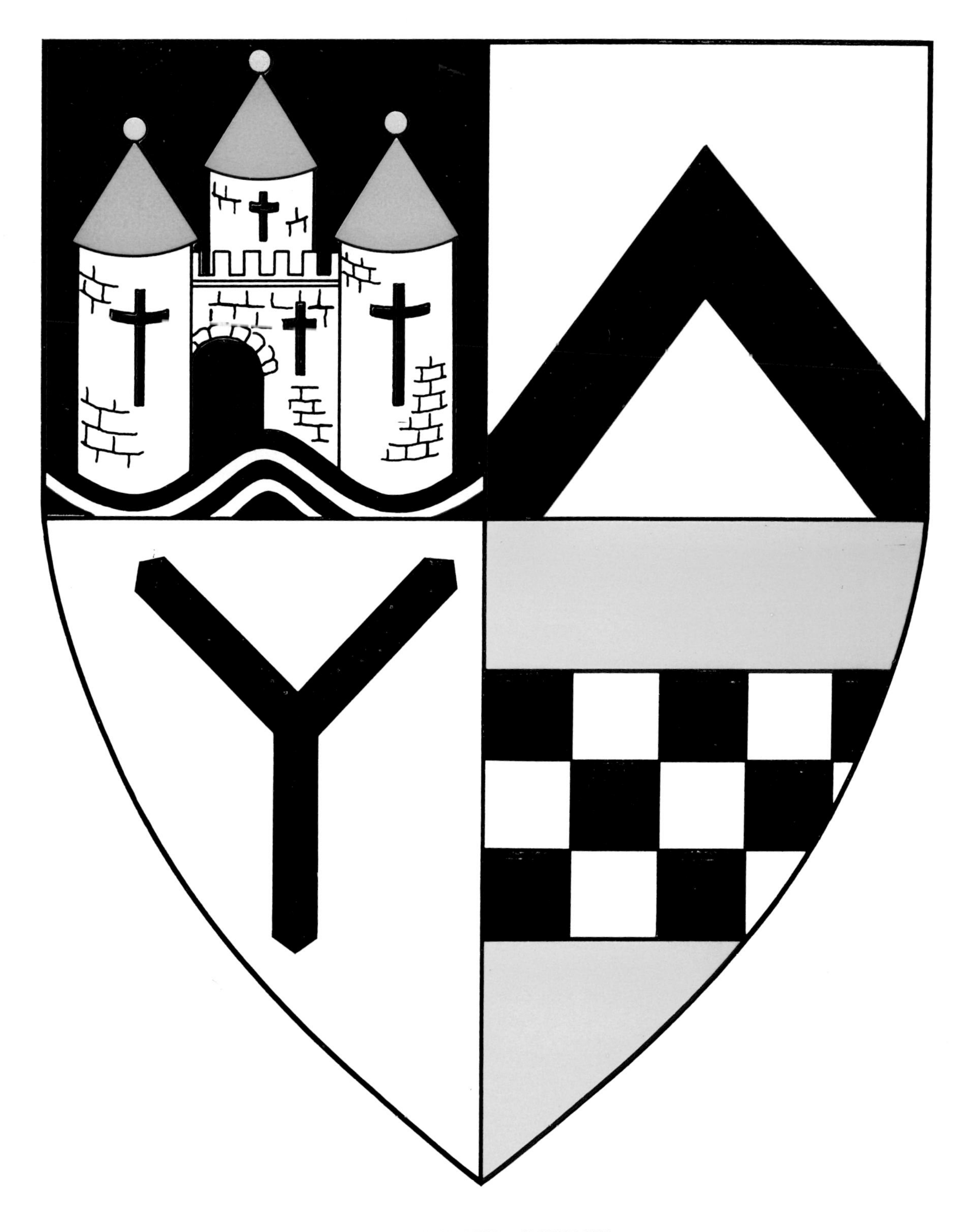

AYR COUNTY COUNCIL

11. COUNTY COUNCIL OF THE COUNTY OF DUNBARTON

"*Argent, a saltire cantoned with four roses Gules, barbed and seeded Vert*".

MOTTO: "*Levenax*".

Dunbarton County Council has simply the arms of the Celtic Earldom of the Lennox, and what an excellent way to perpetuate them. Dunbarton was for centuries a frontier town, first as the capital of the Roman province of Valentia, being the seaport at the western end of Antonine's Wall, and then as capital of the British Kingdom of Strathclyde. The motto of the County Council, "*Levenax*", is a phonetic spelling of the Gaelic *leamhanach* meaning "land of the elm trees" (3). Dunbarton itself is from the Gaelic, *Dun Breatunn* (fort of the Britons). The County Council preferred the original "Dun" spelling, but the town have opted for the more easily pronounced "Dumbarton".

From 870 Dumbarton suffered raids from the Norsemen, none the less in 1222 Alexander II made Dumbarton a royal burgh, fully 40 years before the power of the Norseman was broken at Largs in 1263. It was to Dumbarton Castle that Sir William Wallace was taken after his capture by Sir John Stewart of Menteith in August 1305—later that same month Wallace was accused by Edward I in Westminster Hall and dragged to Smithfield and butchered (13). Bruce built a castle on a rise between the rivers Clyde and Leven, and died at Cardross in 1329, aged 55 years. The earliest Earls of the Lennox were Gaelic, and from this Celtic line come the MacFarlanes. Perhaps the first Earl of Lennox to come readily to mind is Duncan Stewart whose daughter Isobel, unfortunately for Duncan, married Murdoch, Duke of Albany (2nd Regent Albany). This union involved Duncan in plotting against James I, and the end for that for Duncan, and for Murdoch and two of his sons, was at the Heading Hill by Stirling Castle in 1425 (14).

James IV used Dumbarton as his west-coast naval base, and it was from Dumbarton that he sailed to Mingary in Ardnamurchan to receive the submission of the highland chiefs in 1493 and 1495. Mary, Queen of Scots, had many associations with Dumbarton Castle; it was from here that the 6 year old Queen sailed for France in 1548, and it was the Castle of Dumbarton that she sped to via Niddrie Castle, Kirkliston, after her escape from Loch Leven in 1568 (32). Dumbarton Castle was one of the last castles in Scotland held for Mary. After the battle of Langside, however, it was taken from her supporters at the instigation of one of the many Regents during Mary's lifetime — this one was one of her fathers-in-law, Matthew Stewart, 4th Earl of Lennox.

Mary's supporters were led by James Hamilton, 2nd Hamilton Earl of Arran, and the first Regent of the period was James Stewart, Earl of Moray, Mary's half-brother. Moray laid siege to Dumbarton Castle in January 1570, but French ships managed to re-victual the garrison just in time; Moray was assassinated just days after the siege was raised (15, 29). Matthew Stewart, Earl of Lennox, father of the murdered Henry Stewart, Lord Darnley, was next Regent. Lennox chose Thomas Craufurd of Jordanhill (10) as commander of the force to capture the castle, with John Cunningham of Drumquhassil in support. The castle was taken by surprise shortly after dawn on 1st April 1571, though the Governor, Lord Fleming, escaped. John Hamilton, Archbishop of St. Andrew's and half-brother of the 2nd Hamilton Earl of Arran, was not so fortunate, being captured, and hanged at Stirling within the week.

The Flemings were supporters of Bruce, and were rewarded with the forfeited Comyn lands of Kirkintilloch, but built their castle at nearby Cumbernauld (9). The Flemings for a time rose to positions of great influence in the Black Douglas family — a time that came to an abrupt end at the "Black Dinner" in Edinburgh Castle in November 1440.

"Douglas" and "Edinburgh" recall another link with Scotland's past — and present. This time it is with Sir John Hepburn's Regiment (2). Sir John was killed in 1636 and was succeeded by his nephew Sir James Hepburn who was killed in 1637. The command of the regiment then passed in turn to two brothers, Archibald Douglas, 12th Earl of Angus, and Lord James Douglas. In 1653 Louis XIV of France appointed their half-brother Lord George Douglas, as C.O., and in 1675 Charles II created him Earl of Dumbarton — a title with no land to it — but the 1st of Foot became known as Dumbarton's Regiment, and to this day the regimental marchpast is "Dumbarton's Drums". The Earl of Dumbarton was made G.O.C. Scotland by James VII and helped suppress the rising of the 9th Earl of Argyll (the Monmouth Rebellion) (5, 13). The county has close connections with another regiment, The Argyll and Sutherland Highlanders, and Dumbarton Castle latterly served as the Officer's Mess for "Q" (Dumbarton) Battery, 402 (A. & S. H.) Light Regiment, R.A. ,T.A.

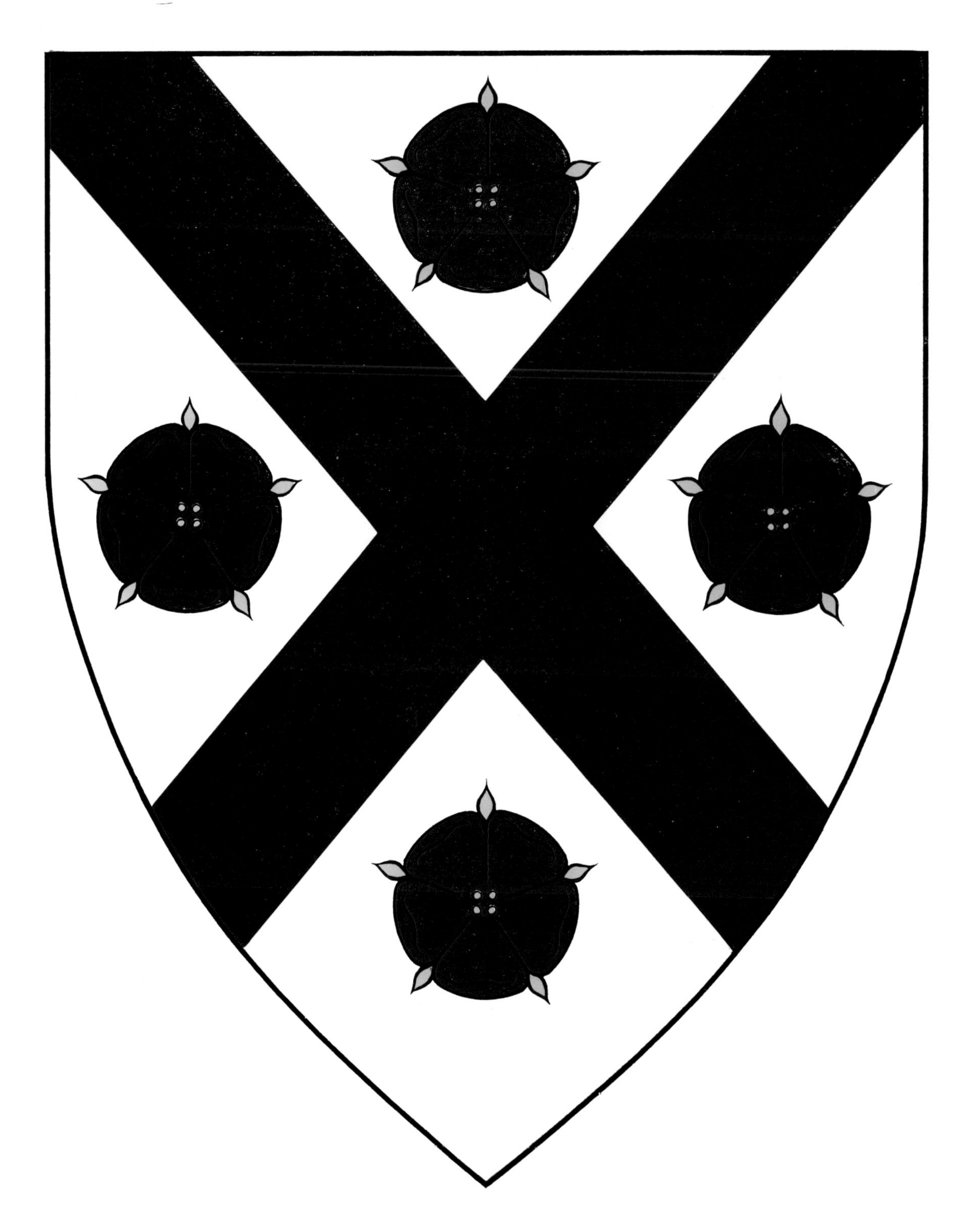

DUNBARTON COUNTY COUNCIL

12. COUNTY COUNCIL OF THE COUNTY OF BUTE

"Parted per pale; on the dexter, parted per fess Gules and Argent, in chief three cinquefoils two and one Ermine, and in base a lymphad sails furled Sable, flagged of the first; and in the sinister, Or, a fess chequy Azure and Argent".

The arms of Bute County Council are interesting on two counts. Firstly they are the first arms in this book to display the galley, and secondly they show a very interesting historical progression.

Somerled had two symbols, one for land and one for sea power — the claymore or the great two-handed sword for power on land and the galley or little ship for power on sea. This little ship, or *naibheag* is very significant. It was half the size of a Viking longship, so making it more manoeuverable; it had a centrally mounted rudder which a longship had not, and it had a fighting top which could hold two or three archers, so increasing the range of the ship's fire power. Virtually all the sons of Somerled, emblazon the galley on their arms. Somerled had three sons: Dougall, who inherited Lorn, Reginald, who inherited Islay, and Angus, who inherited Bute, and the "Rough Bounds". After Angus was killed with his three sons in 1210, his nephew Ruairi — a son of Reginald — seized the "Rough Bounds", while Ruairi's brother Donald — progenitor of the Clan Donald — seized Bute and Arran during the minority of Angus' heiress, his grand-daughter Jean. Bute came into the hands of the family of the High Stewards of Scotland when Jean, heiress of Bute, married Alexander the 4th High Steward. The arms of the Stewarts, the blue and silver fess on its gold field are shown on the sinister half of the County Council's arms. The original Clan Donald castle of Rothesay on the island of Bute was captured by King Haakon of Norway in 1263 on his way to the battle of Largs — a battle in which he was defeated, so ending Norse rule in the Hebrides. Rothesay Castle is thought to have been destroyed by Bruce the following century. The castle was rebuilt, to be again largely destroyed, this time by Cromwell in the 17th century.

The County of Bute comprised not only the Island of Bute and the Cumbraes, but also the Island of Arran. In July 1466 the young King James III was abducted by Robert, Lord Boyd of Kilmarnock. The Boyds, until now, had seldom been in the forefront of Scottish history, but by the end of 1466 Robert Boyd was Regent. One of the things he did was to marry his son Thomas to James III's sister, the Lady Mary, have his son created Earl of Arran and receive the Island of Arran as his bride's dowry. The Boyds' burst to power did not last long, for in 1469 the 18-year old King took the reins of government into his own hands, and the Boyds were declared forfeit. Thomas Boyd and his father went into exile; the Lady Mary returned home to plead the case of her husband, but she stayed in Scotland and married, or she was married to, James, 1st Lord Hamilton. Her son by this marriage, James, 2nd Lord Hamilton, was in 1503 created Earl of Arran, and hence the dexter side of the arms of this County Council the ermine cinquefoils on red of the Hamiltons, and the galley, or *naibheag*, of Somerled, brought back again as the arms of dominion of Arran. The Earl of Arran following James Hamilton, the 3rd Earl was James Stewart, Earl of Arran — this was unusual as the 2nd Hamilton Earl had other sons. James Stewart was murdered by Sir James Douglas at Symontown, Lanarkshire, in 1596. Sir James Douglas' uncle, the 4th Earl of Morton, had been brought to trial and executed, largely at the instigation of James Stewart, Earl of Arran (6).

BUTE COUNTY COUNCIL

13. COUNTY COUNCIL OF THE COUNTY OF RENFREW

"*Azure, a lymphad sail furled Argent, on a shield Or pendant therefrom, a fess chequy of the first and second*".

MOTTO: "*Avito Viret Honore*".

Once again we come across Somerled's galley, and perhaps it is appropriate that here it is shown in ghostly colour. In 1164, Somerled, Lord of the Isles, that immensely important half-Celtic half-Norse historical giant, sailed with his fleet up the rivers Clyde and Cart to Renfrew to meet the king. The night, before the meeting Somerled was murdered in his tent as he slept. His men, leaderless, returned to Islay stopping at Saddell Abbey in Kintyre to bury Somerled's body. This band of men were the forerunners of the Clan Donald.

The "fess chequy" we have seen twice before in this book, and, displayed on a field of gold, it forms the arms of the Norman family who became the High Stewards of Scotland and eventually by marriage found their way to the throne. Paisley Abbey was founded by Walter Fitzalan who came to Scotland with David I in 1141, and was appointed the first High Steward of Scotland in 1160. The Charter founding Paisley Abbey was signed in 1163 at Fotheringay — a place to have ominous implications for a much later member of the Stewart line (26).

Stewarts must figure again in the history of this county, but, first, mention must be made of Sir William Wallace, the Knight of Elderslie. Wallace was born in 1270, and began the resistance to Edward I of England which grew into the War of Scottish Independence, leading to the crowning of Bruce in 1306 (4, 23). Wallace had been captured in 1305, given a mock trial in Westminster Hall, and was hung, drawn and quartered within a month of his arrest (11, 14). The original Paisley Abbey had been destroyed by the English in 1307, and in 1308 the Abbot of Paisley absolved Bruce for the murder of the Red Comyn in 1306 (8).

To go back in time, Alexander, the 4th High Steward, married Jean, great grand-daughter of Somerled, and so came into the possession of Island of Bute. In 1315 Walter, the 6th High Steward married Marjorie, daughter of Robert the Bruce. Marjorie fell from her horse at the Gallowhill, Paisley, in 1316, and was taken to the Abbey where she gave birth to a son, and died aged 23. This son became Robert II, the first of the Royal House of Stewart, and hence Paisley Abbey being known as "the cradle of the Stewart Kings".

Among those buried in the Abbey of Paisley are the six High Stewards, Marjorie Bruce, the two wives of Robert II — Elizabeth Mure and Euphemia of Ross, whose children would vie for the crown, ending in the murder of James I in the Dominican friary at Perth in 1437 — and Robert III, eldest son of Elizabeth Mure of Rowallan. Elizabeth Mure's second son, Robert, became first of the Regent Albanys (14) and her third son, Alexander, won notoriety as the "Wolf of Badenoch" (18, 32). Euphemia of Ross's second son, Walter, Earl of Atholl, got a crown — though not the one of his choosing — in the Grassmarket, Edinburgh in 1437, soon after the murder of James I.

In Paisley Abbey in 1684 John Graham of Claverhouse (Bonnie Dundee/Bloody Claverhouse) married Jean Cochrane of the family of the Cochranes of Dundonald, Ayrshire. The following year 1685, at Blythswood House, downstream from Renfrew ferry, the 9th Earl of Argyll was arrested as he prepared to march on Glasgow; he was brought to trial in Edinburgh for his part in the Monmouth Rebellion (5, 11).

The motto of the County Council is a Stewart one meaning "He flourishes by long-established virtue". It is noteworthy that now the heir-apparent to the crown of Scotland, the Duke of Rothesay, is also styled both the Lord of the Isles, and Baron Renfrew.

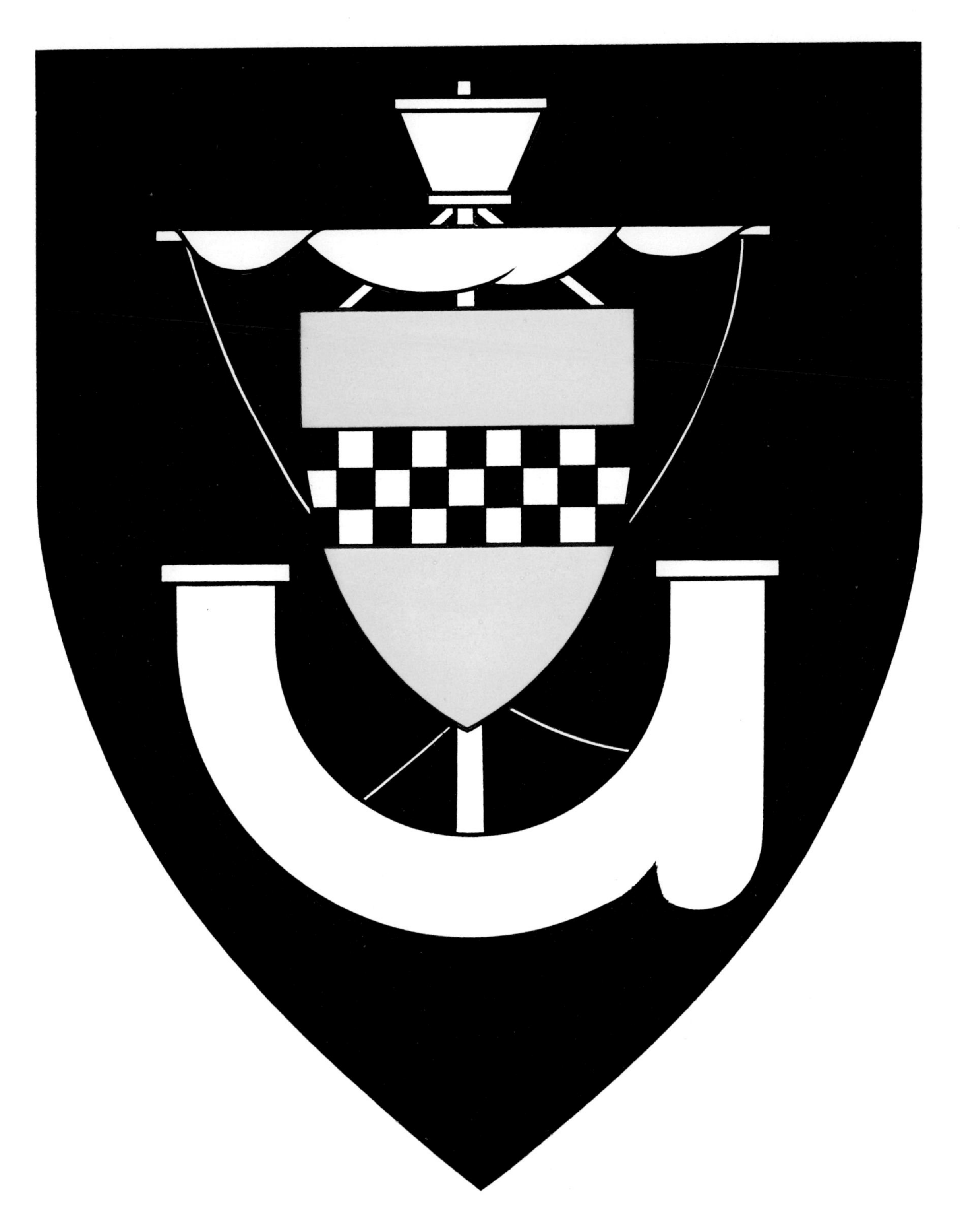

RENFREW COUNTY COUNCIL

14. COUNTY COUNCIL OF THE COUNTY OF STIRLING

"*Azure, on a saltire between two caltraps in chief and base and as many spur rowels in the flanks Argent, a lion rampant Gules, armed and langued of the first*".

The arms of this County Council are nothing if not Scottish, as indeed is fitting for the county containing Bannockburn, the site of Scotland's most devastating victory against the might of all England. The saltire and the lion rampant are clearly Scottish while the caltraps and spur rowels recall the Battle of Bannockburn, 1314. The caltraps were strewn on the ground to cause havoc with the English cavalry; the armoured knights themselves are recalled by the spur rowels. If any of our counties can lay claim to the title "cockpit of Scotland", it is surely Stirlingshire, with battle sites bristling about the county like spear-points from a schiltron—and the battles not just of local importance, but of national significance. September 1297 saw William Wallace defeat an English army at Stirling Bridge — and what an impact Wallace made on Scotland, and in such a short span (13). The outraged Edward I of England, furious at Wallace's declaring Scotland's independence, advanced in person into Scotland and at Falkirk in July 1298, Wallace heavily outnumbered by Edward's army, was defeated, and in 1305 he was captured and taken to Westminster Hall (11). There must have been something about Stirlingshire even then, for Edward I felt drawn to the county again in his later years, but he left it too late and his son had to come in his place.

Edward II came riding at the head of his van of heavily armoured knights, in fact leading an army of around 20,000 men, to relieve Stirling Castle before Midsummer Day 1314. His task seemed quite straightforward, for the way was barred by a Scots army numbering only about 7,000. But numbers are not all that matter, and if this ever needed exemplification, Bruce (31) gave it with salutory finality at Bannockburn. Robert the Bruce's principal captain was Sir James Douglas, the Black Douglas. Through the generations the Black Douglases became so powerful as to vie with the King for authority and successive Scottish Kings sought to curb Black Douglas power by fair means or foul. The 6th Earl of Douglas was murdered in 1440 along with his brother at the Black Dinner in Edinburgh Castle, and in Stirling Castle in 1452 William the 8th Earl was murdered. With the royal castle of Stirling at the hub of the county, and nearby the castle of Doune the home of the Stewart Dukes of Albany, father and son each in turn Regent of Scotland, Stirlingshire could not be described as unexciting. Robert, 1st Duke of Albany, builder of Doune Castle, attempted to arrange the passing of the Earldom of Ross to his second son John, Earl of Buchan, and so precipitated the battle of Harlaw (18, 21). Robert died in the fullness of years in Stirling Castle, and his son Murdoch succeeded him in both the Dukedom and the Regency. This second Regent died at Stirling also, but unlike his father's death, his death was not due to old age, but was by the sword, at the Heading Hill by the Castle in 1425 (11).

By the 17th century the rhythm had changed; the country was again in turmoil and Scotland and indeed Europe were astounded by the light infantry tactics of James Graham, 5th Earl and 1st Marquis Montrose. These tactics were seen with frightful efficiency at the battle of Kilsyth in August 1645, when that terrible combination of Montrose and young Colkitto so mauled General Baillie's army that it ceased to exist as a fighting unit. The blame for the defeat of the Covenant army likely does not rest with Baillie, but with his committee of advisers, whom he could not shake off. In half a dozen years, the tide had turned, and Cromwell's forces led by General Monck took Stirling Castle in 1651 the year after Monck raised his regiment to be known later as the Coldstream Guards (3).

Another century, and another song — and the 18th century gave birth to many songs — Jacobite songs. In Stirlingshire the first Jacobite encounter was not auspicious, for the battle of Sheriffmuir in November 1715 was indecisive and the Jacobite general, the Earl of Mar, did not command confidence. The Hanoverian commander, the Duke of Argyll, had, if anything, the better of the encounter, for Jacobite morale received a perhaps not unexpected blow, and when news reached Scotland of the Jacobite defeat at Preston in Lancashire, that virtually put paid to the 1715 Rising. The next Jacobite action in the county was again wasteful — this time the Jacobite victory at Falkirk, won by a retreating army, an army that had lost its impetus and before long was going to lose about everything else as well — everything but admiration.

Stirling Castle is now the R.H.Q. of The Argyll & Sutherland Highlanders, the regiment formed in 1881 by amalgamation of the 91st Regiment, The Argyllshire Highlanders, with the 93rd Regiment, The Sutherland Highlanders, the latter taking with them to this union their much prized battle honour "Balaclava".

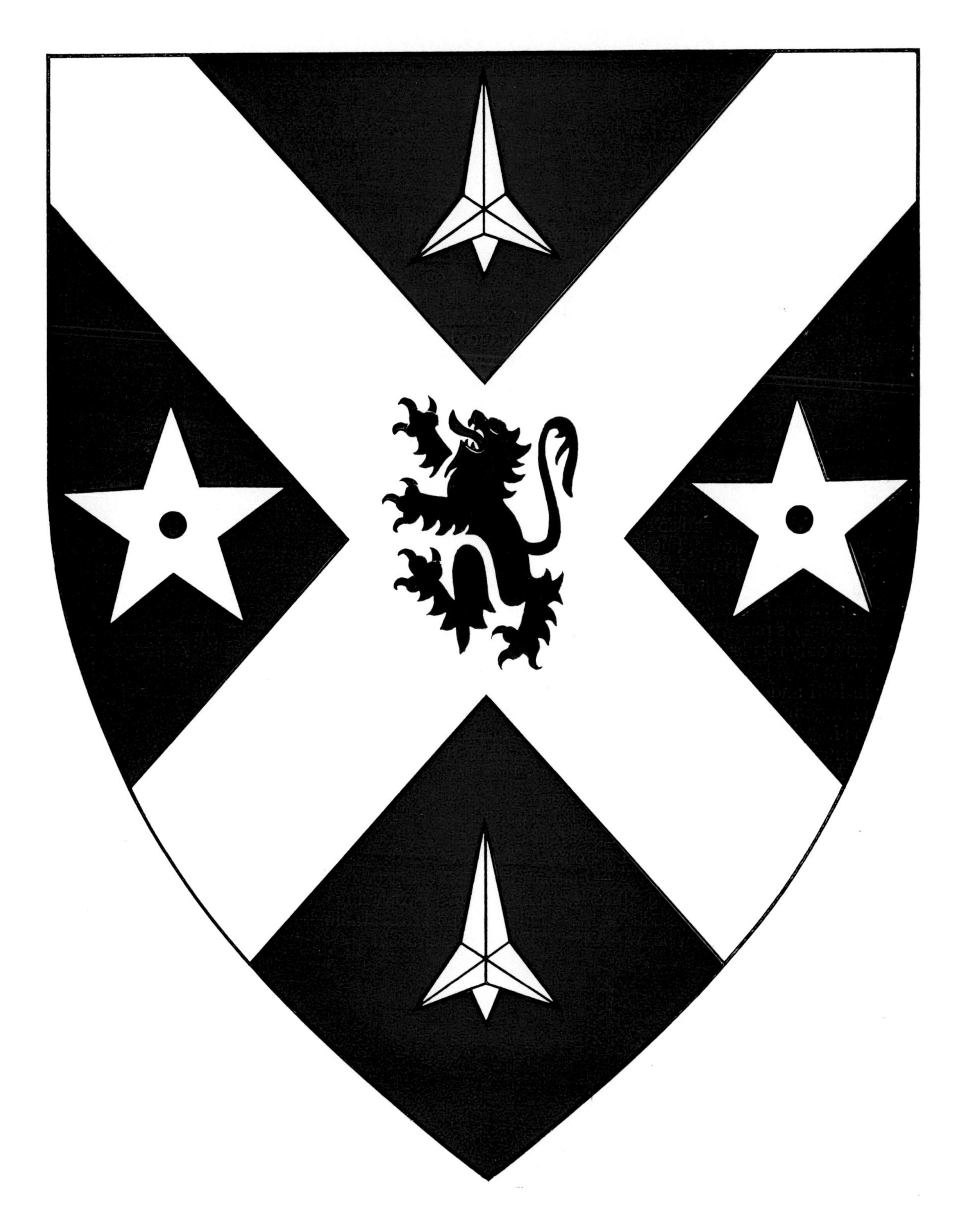

STIRLING COUNTY COUNCIL

15. THE COUNTY COUNCIL OF THE COUNTY OF WEST LOTHIAN

"*Azure, issuant from a mount in base, an oak tree fructed Or, a bordure Argent charged with four gillyflowers Gules, alternately with as many laurel leaves slipped Vert*".

The arms of West Lothian County Council reflect mainly the family of Livingstone, who at one time held the Earldom of Linlithgow (the county town of West Lothian) and also of Callendar (cf. Callendar House, Falkirk). The Livingstones, Earls of Linlithgow, in token of the Earldom of Linlithgow, superimposed a small shield — an escutcheon — on their family arms. This escutcheon bore a gold oak tree growing from a golden base, set against a blue background, all surrounded by a silver border charged with eight red gillyflowers. In the arms of the County Council the number of gillyflowers has been reduced and laurel leaves introduced alternately. The laurel leaves — or rather the laurel leaf — is from the arms of the Hope family, Earls of Hoptoun in the county, whose seat Hoptoun House is one of the architectural treasures of Scotland. Linlithgow was the site in 1570 of the assassination of James Stewart "the Good Earl of Moray" (11, 29).

Blackness, on the Firth of Forth, was once one of Scotland's main ports; its castle was built in the 15th century and was added to appreciably thereafter. In the 17th century, it was used as a prison for Covenanters. Blackness Castle was garrisoned by the French in 1548 when a contingent from France came over to aid the Mary, Queen of Scots faction. When Mary fled to England in 1568 the keeper, or captain, of the castle, Alexander Stewart, initially held out, but eventually changed sides, surrendered the castle to the Regent, and so retained the captaincy of the castle. Almost 30 years later the captaincy passed to the Livingstones, but the castle was taken from them by General George Monck, of Coldstream Guards fame, in 1654. Not far away stands The Binns, the construction of which also dates from the 15th century, and which also has strong connections with the persecutors of the Covenanters. At one time an underground passage linked The Binns with Blackness Castle.

The Binns is renowned as being the home of General Sir Tam Dalyell, and so links The Binns with Scotland's only regular cavalry regiment to be still — after a fashion — in the British Army's Order of Battle, The Royal Scots Greys (2nd Dragoon Guards) — second to none. The Greys' formal history starts in 1681 and right from the beginning they were a royal regiment; in fact, The Royal Regiment of Scotch Dragoons. The first C.O. was Tam Dalyell of The Binns, a Royalist like Montrose, and one who had been imprisoned by Cromwell in the Tower of London for military activities in Ireland against the Parliamentarians. Subsequently Tam Dalyell entered the service of Czar Alexis of Russia, where his service was recognised by promotion to General, and eventually Charles II recalled him and appointed him G.O.C. Scotland, with specific responsibility for putting down the forces of what was now the Solemn League and Covenant. The main stronghold of the Covenant was in south-west Scotland, and the task of suppressing the Covenanters had been grimly started by three troops of dragoons — the forerunners of the Greys — led by John Graham of Claverhouse, Viscount Dundee — "Bloody Claverhouse" or "Bonnie Dundee" — depending if the reader be lowland or highland. Over the years The Scots Greys had the unique authority from the Lord Lyon King of Arms to fly the Royal Scottish Banner. The Greys in July 1971 amalgamated with the 3rd Carabiniers to become The Royal Scots Dragoon Guards — a union performed with "Amazing Grace".

WEST LOTHIAN COUNTY COUNCIL

16. COUNTY COUNCIL OF THE COUNTY OF PERTH

"*Or, a lion rampant Gules, armed and langued Azure, standing on a compartment Proper and brandishing in his dexter forepaw a scimitar of the last, all within a double tressure flory counterflory of the second; on a dexter chief canton of the third a front view of the Palace of Scone, Argent, ensigned on the top with an imperial crown Proper*".

MOTTO: "*Pro Lege et Libertate*".

Perth County Council was one of only three of our County Councils to have had supporters, and one of only six to have had a crest. The motto translated reads "For Law and Liberty".

The arms are strongly reminiscent of the Royal Arms of Dominion of Scotland — they are also reminiscent of the arms of the Royal Banner Bearer. Perthshire has of course, strong links with the Scottish throne, one of the dynasties indeed, the House of Dunkeld, being of the county. The imperially crowned Palace of Scone reminds one of the time when Perth was once the capital of Scotland and many Kings of Scots were crowned there, including in 1306 Robert the Bruce (8, 23). It was from Scone that the Stone of Destiny was looted by Edward I of England and taken to Westminster Abbey.

Perthshire has for long been renowned as the home of The Black Watch, "the 42nd", The Royal Highland Regiment. The Black Watch is the senior highland regiment, being raised by adding four additional companies to the six independent companies raised by the government in 1725. 1725 was not the beginning of the Watches, however; Watches had been organised as local independent *vigilante* groups some time before that. In 1681 Thomas Gorrie, of Culnacloich, was captain of the Logiealmond Watch — which appears to be one of the earliest Watch companies of which there is record. The companies wore dark tartans and they become known as the "Black Watch" in contrast with the "Redcoats".

There is record of a George Patton in Culnacloich by about 1750. There is evidence to suggest that Captain George Patton, A.D.C. to General John Pershing during the 1st World War , was of this line. George Patton survived the 1st World War to play a not inconsiderable part in the 2nd World War, as General George S. Patton, U.S. Army.

Perthshire is also the birthplace of another regiment of great note. This other regiment started off life as the 90th Perthshire Volunteers (Light Infantry), and was raised at Perth in May 1794 by Thomas Graham of Balgowan. The story behind that is a tale in itself. Thomas Graham rose to the rank of Lieutenant-General and was created Lord Lynedoch; he was the victor of Barrosa in the Peninsular campaign (1811). In 1881 the 90th Perthshire Light Infantry became the 2nd Battalion Scottish Rifles with the marchpast "The Gathering of the Grahams"; the regiment was disbanded in 1968 (7, 8). Appropriately, the regimental club in Glasgow is in Lynedoch Place. It is interesting to note that The Cameronians were first blooded at Dunkeld within months of their formation, when they put up a very stout and successful defence against highlanders following up their success at Killiecrankie in July 1689, i.e. they were first blooded in the county with whose volunteers they were in the future to unite. In 1806 Lord Lynedoch sold part of his estate, The Cairnies, to James Patton, Sheriff-Clerk of Perthshire. In 1844 The Cairnies was gifted by the Pattons to the Scottish Episcopal Church for the building of Trinity College, Glenalmond.

In 1900, during the Boer War, 1899-1902, members of the Caledonian Society of Johannesburg suggested the raising of a corps of Scotsmen in South Africa to be called "The Scottish Horse". Lord Kitchener, G.O.C.-in-C., readily agreed, and the task of raising the unit, and its command, were given to the Marquis of Tullibardine. Such was the birth of The Scottish Horse, and in the course of time the R.H.Q. became Dunkeld. During the 2nd World War The Scottish Horse served as the 79th and 80th Medium Regiments, Royal Artillery.

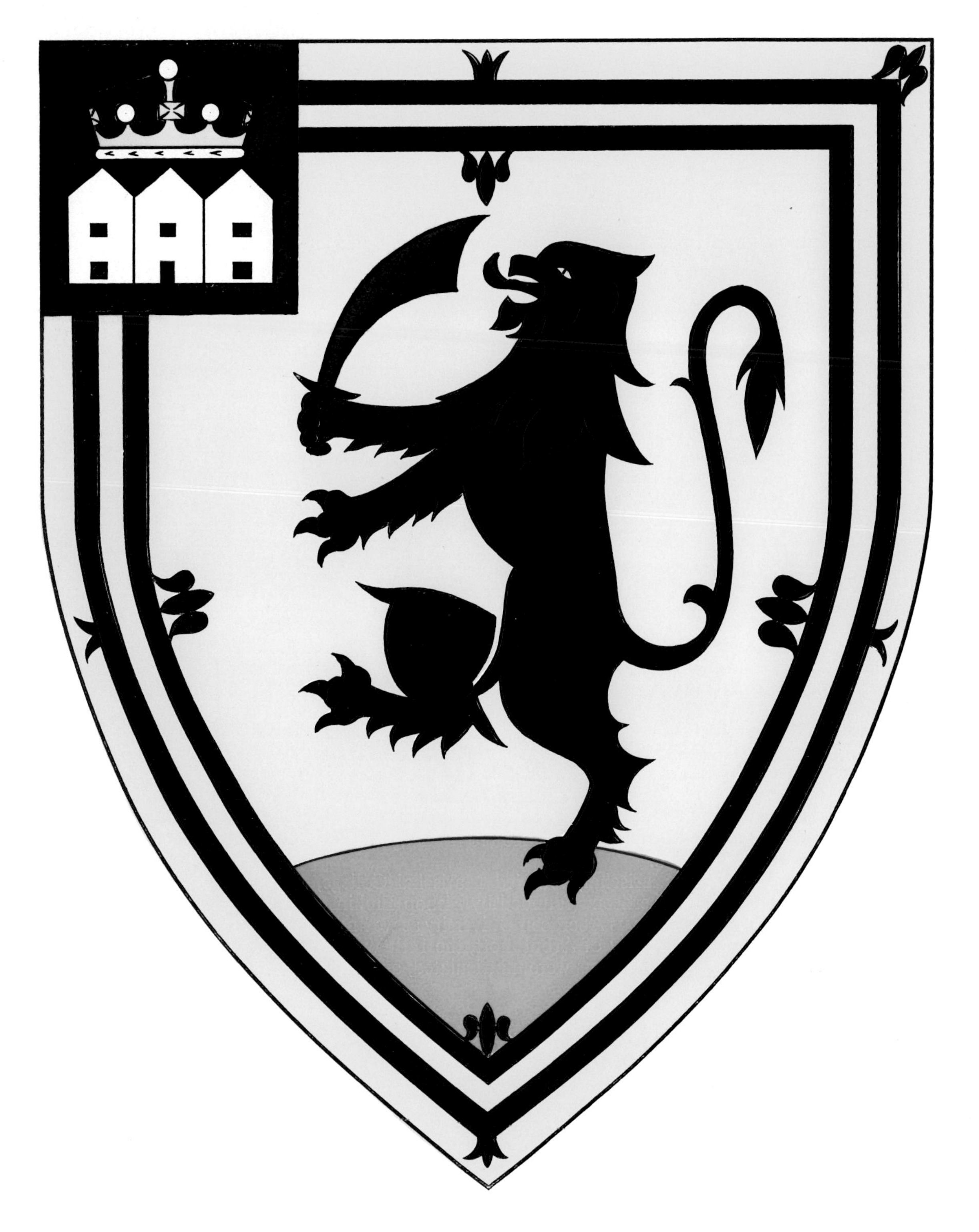

PERTH COUNTY COUNCIL

17. COUNTY COUNCIL OF THE COUNTY OF KINCARDINE

"*Gules, the Sword of State and Sceptre of Scotland in saltire, in chief the Crown of Scotland, and in base on a rock a ruined castle all Or*".

MOTTO: "*Laus Deo*".

This County Council's arms are both simple and dramatic. They tell of the saving of the Honours of Scotland in Dunottar Castle, seat of the Earls Marischal, from Cromwell's army. William Keith, the 6th Earl Marischal, was a Covenanter, but in 1651, after the coronation at Scone of Charles II, he brought the Scottish Regalia to Dunottar Castle for safe-keeping. Dunottar Castle was besieged and the chances of its holding out long enough were slim, so with the collaboration of the castle governor, George Ogilvy of Barras, and Christian Fletcher, the wife of the minister of Kinneff Parish Kirk, James Granger, the Honours of Scotland were smuggled out, to be buried under the church's floor. They remained there until after the Restoration of the Monarchy in 1660.

The meaning of Kincardine is not certain, but perhaps the most likely derivation is from the Gaelic "*ceann-garadh*" meaning head-dyke, or head-garden. The suggestion "head-dyke" could refer to the hills to the west hemming in the Howe of the Mearns, and the Howe of the Mearns is indeed a garden. Again, *garadh*, meaning a dyke, could refer to the coastal cliffs.

To the north of the county on the Hill of Fare in 1562 was fought the battle of Corrichie, when Mary, Queen of Scots, subdued the Gordons led by the Earl of Huntly. Mary's G.O.C. was her half-brother, Lord James Stewart, and after the royalist victory, Mary created him Earl of Moray (11, 29). South from the Hill of Fare and down by the river Dee stands the older of the two castles of Durris and here Edward I of England lodged in July 1296 during a punitive foray into Scotland. Indeed it was on his way north, in March 1296, that he caused the notorious Sack of Berwick. In his advance Edward of England went as far north as Elgin, having on his way captured Edinburgh Castle, and so publically humiliated John Balliol at Strathcathro Kirk in early July, that "Toom Tabard" virtually abdicated less than a week later at Brechin. On his return journey to England, Edward called at Scone, from where he stole the Stone of Destiny (16), which, apart from a brief interlude 1950-1951, has remained in Westminster Abbey.

Balbegno Castle, just south of Fettercairn, was built in 1570 by James Wood, a descendant of James IV's famous admiral, Andrew Wood of Largo in Fife. Captain Andrew Wood, in his ship the "Yellow Caravel", and commanding a Scottish squadron, defeated an English fleet in the Firth of Forth in 1489, ending up by capturing the English admiral and three of his ships, off the Tay Estuary. James IV knighted Andrew Wood and made him captain of the pride of the Scottish fleet the "Great Michael". When James IV sailed from Dumbarton to Mingary in 1495, command of the naval squadron was vested in Sir Andrew Wood.

George Keith 4th Earl Marischal, founded Marischal College, Aberdeen, in 1593. Marischal College and King's College, Aberdeen, (founded by Bishop Elphinstone, Chancellor of Scotland, in 1494) were united in 1860, to give us Aberdeen University as we know it today.

The motto is that of the family of Arbuthnott, the 14th Viscount of Arbuthnott being the Lord Lieutenant of the county when the arms were matriculated, and on translation reads "Praise to God".

KINCARDINE COUNTY COUNCIL

18. COUNTY COUNCIL OF THE COUNTY OF ABERDEEN

"Quarterly: 1st, Azure, three garbs Or; 2nd, Azure, a bend between six cross-crosslets fitchée Or; 3rd, Or, a fess chequy Azure and Argent between three open crowns Gules; 4th, Azure, three boars' heads couped Or".

No county council's arms could have more history in them than Aberdeen's. The first quarter displays the arms of the ancient Earldom of Buchan, a possession for long of the Comyn (Cumming) family who obtained it by marrying a Buchan heiress. Indeed, the three "garbs" or sheaves may well be sheaves of the herb cummin and so the charges of the first quarter may well be an heraldic pun. The Comyn family at one time must have been one of Scotland's most powerful, with lands from Lochaber in the west to Buchan and Angus in the east and Galloway in the south and, in between, Badenoch, the Lennox, Clydesdale (Dalserf) and Menteith. Their castles included; Balvenie, Dalswinton, Dundarg, Ellon, Inveralochy, Inverlochy, Inverugie, Kirkintilloch, Loch-an-eilean, Lochindorb, Rattray, Slains, Tarradale and Wigtown. The misfortune of the Comyns was that they opposed Bruce who eventually subdued the family in the fearful herschip of Buchan in 1308.

The second quarter displays the arms of the ancient Earldom of Mar, an Earldom associated with two Erskine families even to this day, the Earls of Mar, and the Earls of Mar and Kellie. Those shown in the second quarter are the arms of dominion of Mar — the third quarter shows the arms of Alexander Stewart of Strathavon (25), who became Earl of Mar in 1404. This Stewart Earl of Mar was an illegitimate son of Alexander Stewart, Earl of Buchan, more widely known as the "Wolf of Badenoch". It was this Stewart Earl of Mar who opposed Donald of Islay at Harlaw in 1411. One of the Lord of the Isles' captains to fall at Harlaw was Hector MacLean of Duart, known as Red Hector of the Battles, and it was the death of this Duart chief that gave rise to the MacLean slogan "Another for Hector!"

The fourth quarter is for the Gordons, who like the Comyns and Stewarts are of Norman origin. The family's first settlement in Scotland was at Huntly in the parish of Gordon in Berwickshire, but they moved north when Sir Adam, Lord of Gordon, was granted the lands and Lordship of Strathbogie by Robert I (the Bruce). After the forfeiture of the Lordship of the Isles, the Gordons, as Earls and Marquises of Huntly, Aberdeenshire (29), soon moved to the forefront of Scottish history, calling themselves "Cocks of the North". The Gordons supplied Montrose with the bulk of his cavalry for his unparallelled campaigns of the 17th century. The crest and motto of the chief of the Gordons became the cap-badge of The Gordon Highlanders, a regiment that from the beginning never wanted for recruits, thanks initially to the Duchess of Gordon, wife of the 4th Duke of Gordon whose son, the Marquis of Huntly, raised the second battalion as the 100th Highland Regiment (later the 92nd) in 1794. In their first campaign two men of the 92nd saved the life of General John Moore during the battle of Egmont-on-Zee, in Holland, in 1799. When General Moore was later knighted, he chose as one of his supporters a Gordon Highlander. After Sir John Moore was killed in action at Corunna in 1809, The Gordon Highlanders put black buttons on their spats in his memory.

Aberdeen has also contributed to contemporary heraldic usage; at the outbreak of the 2nd World War a tactical sign was required for the new Anti-Aircraft Command, and the question was debated at Bently Priory, the London home of the Earl of Aberdeen. Someone noticed the crest of the 4th Earl of Aberdeen over the doorway — a drawn bow — and from this came the familiar Royal Artillery A.A. shoulder flash, a black drawn cross-bow pointing upwards, on a red ground.

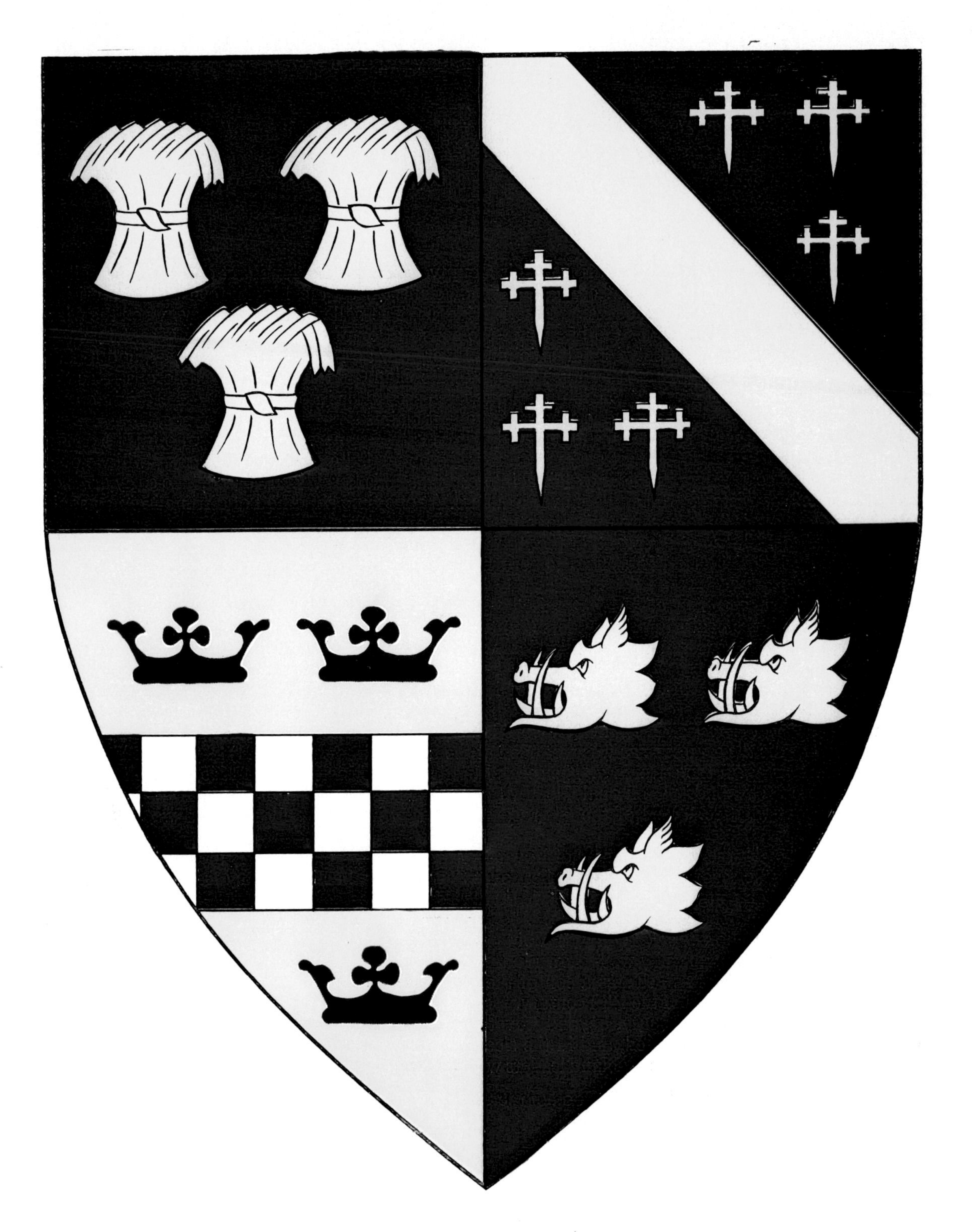

ABERDEEN COUNTY COUNCIL

19. COUNTY COUNCIL OF THE COUNTY OF INVERNESS

"*Azure, in dexter chief a stag's head and in sinister chief a bull's head both erased, and in base a galley, sails furled, oars in action and flagged, all Or*".

MOTTO: "*Air son Math na Siorrachd*".

Simple, bold and telling are the arms of this County Council. The dominant charge is the galley, representing the Clan Chattan, that confederation of clans led by the Mackintosh and comprising originally the Macphersons, Macbeans and the Davidsons. The galley recalls the days when the Clan Chattan aligned themselves under the banner of the sons of Somerled, Lords of the Isles. The early lands of the Clan Chattan lay between a line joining Invergarry and Inverlochy in the east, and Morar and Knoydart in the west. The southern neighbours of the Clan Chattan were the Camerons — as the Camerons expanded northwards the Clan Chattan were eased over into Badenoch. The origin of the name Cameron is perhaps obscure; one school of thought claims the name is indigenous, being Gaelic for " crooked nose", whilst another school of thought cites the Camerons of Ballegarno in Fife as the origin. This latter theory claims that a Cameron from Fife married a Lochaber heiress — will we ever know for sure? The Fife hypothesis is certainly interesting, and is heraldically based. The early arms of the Earls of Fife consisted of red and gold vertical bars. At one time a method of distinguishing a son's arms from those of his father was to turn the father's arms on their side — and this gives the arms of the Camerons of Lochiel. In addition to that the Lochaber Camerons used to quarter a lion rampant, the device used by later Earls of Fife. The Camerons also used to quarter the galley of Somerled, the *naibheag*.

In 1793 Alan Cameron of Erracht raised the 79th Regiment, or Cameron Highlanders, now amalgamated with the Seaforth Highlanders (29) to form the Queen's Own Highlanders. The march-past of The Queen's Own Cameron Highlanders was "Pibroch of Donald Dhu", recalling a battle of long ago — the first battle of Inverlochy in 1431 — when Donald Dhu Balloch defeated the King's army, led by the Earl of Mar, in vengeance for imprisoning his cousin, Alexander, Lord of the Isles. (The march "Pibroch of Donald Dhu" is not really a pibroch, but is derived from one, whose earliest name in translation is "Black Donald Balloch of the Isles' March to the first battle of Inverlochy"). This Earl of Mar is the same one as was wounded at the battle of Harlaw (18, 21) 20 years before, when Clan Donald was again the adversary, The second battle of Inverlochy was in 1645 when the bulk of the troops were yet again of Clan Donald, led by the Marquis of Montrose and Alasdair — Colkitto — when they swept what remained of the Clan Campbell army into the February-cold waters of Loch Linnhe.

The stag's head is the crest of Fraser of Lovat — *MacShimi* — and as such is the cap-badge of The Lovat Scouts. In the second World War The Lovat Scouts served as a specially trained ski battalion and many of the regiment volunteered for service in the Commandos, as indeed did the present *MacShimi*, Simon Fraser, Brigadier The Lord Lovat, D.S.O., M.C. The Lovat Scouts are still in being as "A" Company, 2nd Battalion 51st (Highland) Volunteers, T.A.V.R. The bull's head is the crest of the MacLeods of MacLeod, a family well-known in the west, whose seat is Dunvegan Castle on the Isle of Skye. The original Leod was perhaps a son of the Norseman, Olav the Black, King of Man and the North Isles, around the turn of the 12th century.

Over to the east of the county, beyond Lovat, lies Drumossie Moor where, in 1746, the Jacobite cause in Scotland blazed, flickered, and in the sleet and snow of an April morning at Culloden, went out, and the fears of many of the highland leaders were realised.

The Gaelic motto reads "For the Good of the County".

INVERNESS COUNTY COUNCIL

20. COUNTY COUNCIL OF THE COUNTY OF NAIRN

"*Or, on a chevron Gules, between two water-bougets in chief and in base a stag's head cabossed Sable, three mullets Argent*".

MOTTO: "*Unite and be Mindful*".

Crisp and sharp are the arms of the County Council of Nairn. The Calders were the ancient rulers or thanes of Calder; in 1494 John, the 7th Thane, married Isobel, daughter of Rose of Kilravock. John and Isobel had but one child, Muriel, born posthumously, and it was the intention of infant Muriel's maternal grandfather to marry her to his grandson and heir, so linking again the families of Calder and Rose. The Justice General of Scotland had other ideas. Muriel's grandfather, Rose of Kilravock, had fallen foul of the law — in short he was in trouble. The Justice General, who happened to be the Earl of Argyll, would smooth the path if he could have Muriel's hand for one of his kinsmen. And so it came about, against fierce Calder resistance, that Muriel was carried off by Campbell of Inverliever, on Loch Awe-side, to be married to the third son of the 2nd Earl of Argyll. Six of Campbell's seven sons were killed in this abduction, but Sir John Campbell of Argyll married his childbride, heiress of the Thanes of Calder, in 1510. He and his family henceforword styled themselves Campbells of Calder (or Cawder). The stag's head on the County Council's arms recalls the Calder family, anciently Thanes of Calder. The background colour and the two water bougets are from the arms of the Roses of Kilravock.

The red chevron is from the arms of Brodie of Brodie, and the silver five-pointed stars are from the arms of the Baillies of Lochloy. The motto is a fusion of the motto of Brodie of Brodie, "Unite" with that of Campbell of Cawdor, "Be mindful", which is in turn a variation of the motto of Campbell of Argyll, which is "*Ne obliviscaris*".

The Campbells of Calder had not left Argyll for good when they took themselves up to the north-east. After the battle of Gruinart in 1598 James VI decided to dispossess the family of MacDonald of Islay (now of Dunivaig) (22) and allowed the Earl of Argyll to establish his kinsman, Sir John Campbell of Calder, brother-in-law of the Sir James MacDonald of Dunivaig, who had been outlawed, on Islay. This cost Sir John Campbell of Calder dearly, as he had to sell part of his north east-lands and mortgage other parts to give himself the funds with which to fight his way into Islay. Campbell of Calder received a Royal Charter for Islay c. 1621, and the family remained in possession until Sir Hugh Campbell of Calder sold it to Daniel Campbell of Shawfield in 1726. In 1853 Islay was sold by Walter F. Campbell of Shawfield to James Morrison of Basildon, Berkshire.

The castle of Brodie is just outside the county on the east side, and just within the county on the west side is Kilravock Castle. Between the two lies Auldearn site of a typical Montrose/young Colkitto victory against a Covenant army commanded by General Sir John Hurry, in May 1645. Montrose was also the tactician behind the defeat of another Covenant General, this time a Nairnshire man, William Baillie of Letham, whose army was routed by the combination of Montrose and Alasdair at Kilsyth in August 1645 (14).

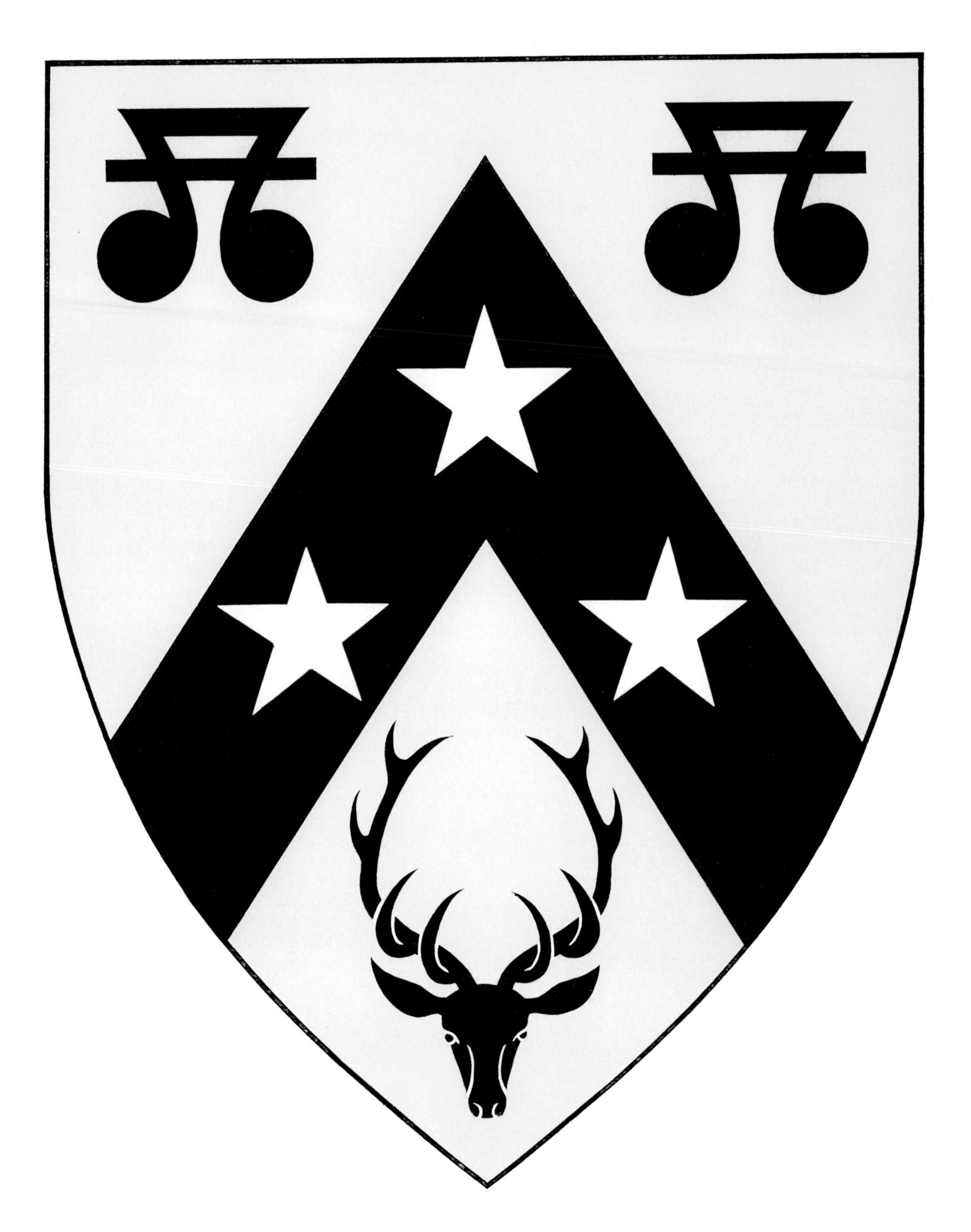

NAIRN COUNTY COUNCIL

21. COUNTY COUNCIL OF THE COUNTY OF ROSS AND CROMARTY

"Per fess and in base per pale; 1st, Gules, three lions rampant Argent; 2nd, Azure, a stag's head cabossed Or, 3rd, Or, a beacon Azure, masoned Argent, enflamed Gules".

MOTTO: "*Dread God and Do Well*".

Across the top of this county's arms stand the defiant rampant lions of the ancient Earldom of Ross, the Earldom that was the root cause of "the Red Harlaw" in 1411. There can be few more fascinating family trees than those twining and coiling around the Earldom of Ross. Alexander Leslie, Earl of Ross, died in Dingwall in 1402, leaving his only child, Euphemia Leslie, as his heiress. Euphemia's mother was Isobel Stewart, daughter of Robert Stewart, 1st Duke of Albany — the first Regent Albany. What exactly happened to this Euphemia is not known, but an agreement had been made in 1370 stating that if Euphemia had no children, or was done away with (far-sighted people that drew up that agreement!), then the next in line would be her aunt Margaret Leslie, sister of the late Earl. One way, or another, Regent Albany persuaded Euphemia to renounce her rights of Ross in favour of Albany's second son, Euphemia's uncle, John Stewart, Earl of Buchan (14). Now it so happened that Margaret Leslie was married to a very powerful person in Donald II of Islay, Lord of the Isles. It is of further interest to note that Donald of Islay's mother was Lady Margaret Stewart, a sister of Regent Albany. The Lord of the Isles did not like the way things were going and he challenged his uncle the Regent and marched on Aberdeen. Before setting off on this mission the Lord of the Isles augmented the *naibheag* on his banner by stringing up from the galley's mast the eagle supporter of the arms of the Earls of Ross. At Harlaw, north-east of Aberdeen, he was opposed by his cousin, Alexander Stewart, Earl of Mar, in late July. The most interesting comment on the outcome of this battle is perhaps the heraldic one — "the Harlaw augmentation" — on the arms of MacVurich, the sennachie of the Lord of the Isles, registered in the Court of the Irish Heralds in Dublin.

Ross momentarily claimed the stage of Scottish history earlier than Harlaw, though the repercussion of this brief appearance is not seen until 26 years after that battle. Robert the Bruce's sister, the Lady Maud, married Hugh, 4th Earl of Ross and Sheriff of Cromarty, and through this marriage the earldom descended. On the death of the Lady Maud, Hugh married again, this time Margaret Graham, and by her he had a son Hugh, progenitor of the Clan Ross, and a daughter Euphemia. We have met this Euphemia of Ross already (13), for she it was who married Robert II, and the offspring of this marriage were both the instigators and perpetrators of the murder of James I in an ill-fated bid to gain the crown.

The stag's head is none other than the *cabarfeidh* of the MacKenzies of Kintail, who became Earls of Seaforth. The *cabarfeidh* shield charge of the MacKenzies became famous as the cap-badge of the Seaforth Highlanders, and now is incorporated in the cap-badge of the Queen's Own Highlanders (Seaforth and Camerons) (29).

The flaming beacon recalls both the crest of the MacKenzies and the shield charge of the MacLeods of Lewis: coincidentally it also reminds the writer of a well- known MacCrimmon pibroch with strong Kintail connections — "Squinting Patrick's Flame of Wrath". The motto is derived from a combination of the motto of the Munros "Dread God" and the Urquharts "Mean Well, Speak Well, and Do Well".

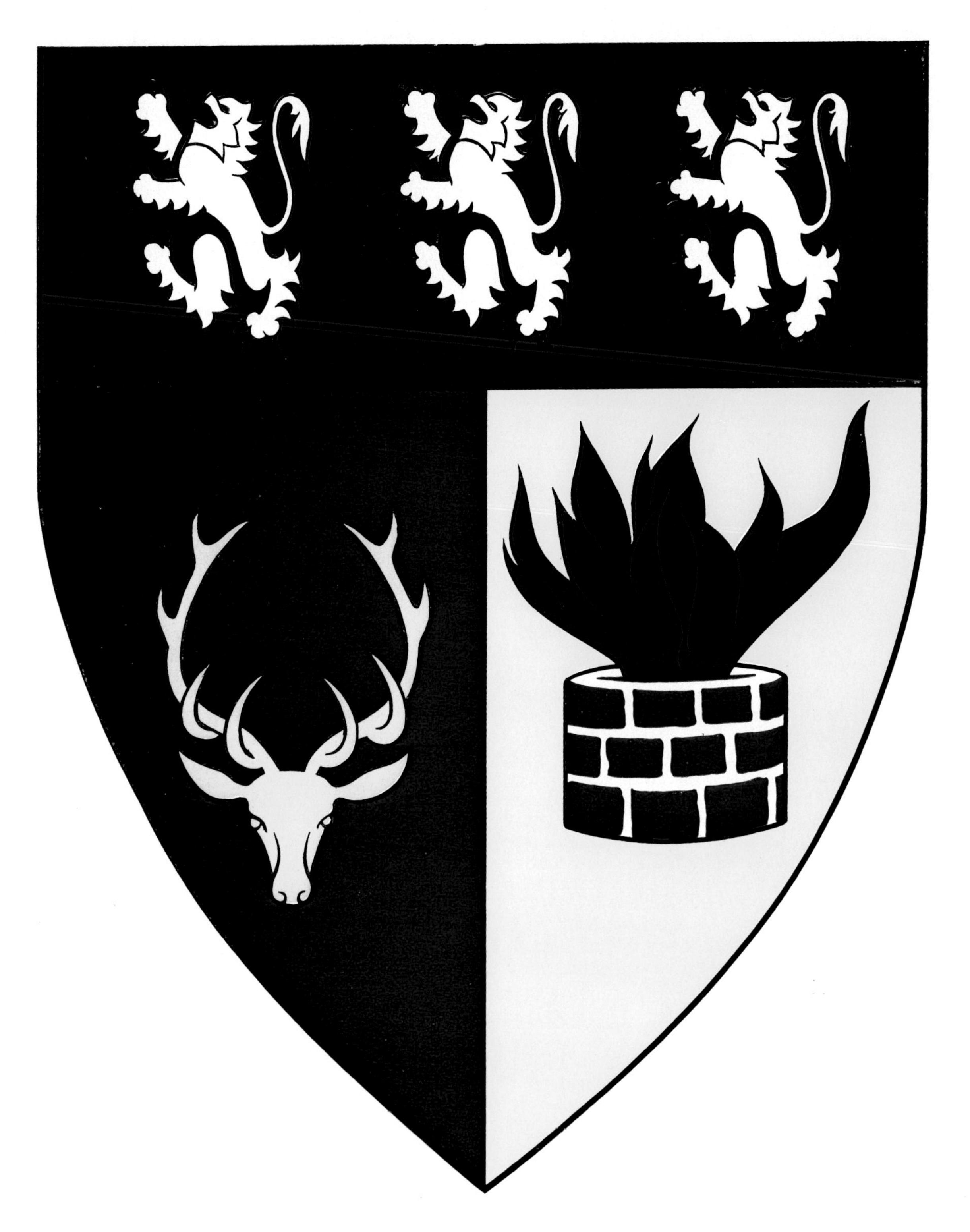

ROSS & CROMARTY COUNTY COUNCIL

22. COUNTY COUNCIL OF THE COUNTY OF ARGYLL

"*Parted per fess and in chief per pale; 1st, gyronny of eight Or and Sable; 2nd, Or, a wing displayed Gules, claw membered Sable, grasping a sword in pale Azure, hilted and pommelled Argent, and environed of an antique crown also Gules; in base Argent, a galley, oars in action, sails furled Sable, with a beacon enflamed Gules at the masthead; over all a fess wavy Azure charged with a bar wavy Argent, upon the last five fish naiant Gules*".

MOTTO: "*Seas ar Coir*".

History is here! The wavy central division with the fish signifies the importance of fishing to this county. Of the other three charges, two have direct connections with Somerled (12), and the other with Clan *Duibhne*, the Campbells. The gyronny of eight is the family charge of the Campbells, and appears in one form or another in virtually all Campbell arms. The Campbells fought for Bruce at Bannockburn (14) and Archibald Campbell, 2nd Earl of Argyll fell at Flodden (3).

The winged-blade is an ancient device and was the insignia of Somerled's admiral, whose name *Mac-sgiath-linn* or MacSgilling means "son of the winged blade". The sword is Somerled's symbol for power on land, and the crown that of the Lordship of the Isles. MacSgilling was a Galloway man, perhaps a kinsman of Alan MacDowall, Lord of Galloway. Galloway may have contributed more to the heraldry of Argyll than just the "winged blade", for it is thought by some that the first Dougall's mother was a MacDowall of Galloway, and this if so, could explain the silver lion, uncrowned, on its blue field on the arms of the MacDougalls of Lorn (9, 26). MacDougall and MacDowall are essentially the same word, being *Mac-dubh-gall*, "son of the dark stranger".

The galley, or *naibheag* (from which Dunivaig Castle on Islay — *Dun-naibheag*), is interesting; the arms of dominion of the Lordship of Lorn were the same as of the Lordship of the Isles — a black galley on a gold field — but with the difference that the fighting top was shown in flames and called a beacon. Such are the quarterings today of the MacDougalls of Dunollie whose forebears were Lords of Lorn. The Lordship of Lorn is presently in the Campbell of Argyll family, and the quartering the Campbells wear for Lorn, is a black galley on a silver field — and no beacon. Between the MacDougall Lords of Lorn and the Campbell Lords of Lorn, another family held the Lordship. The name is scarcely surprising, bearing in mind that the MacDougalls supported Balliol; the other family were of course the Stewart Lords of Lorn. One Stewart coat has been noted with a black galley on a silver field "with St. Anthony's fire on the topmast" — maybe this is the link between the black galley with beacon on a gold field and the black galley without beacon on a silver field. The Stewarts of Appin are descendants of the Stewart Lords of Lorn.

Raw materials from Argyll played a major part in the Napoleonic Wars; the bulk of the British bullets fired at Waterloo were made from lead mined at Strontian, and cannon balls for Nelson's fleet were made at Lorn Furnace, Taynuilt. Indeed it is at Taynuilt that the first memorial was erected in Britain to Admiral Nelson, following the Battle of Trafalgar in 1805. Another product of importance in the Napoleonic War effort that came from Argyll and other coasts was kelp, a seaweed rich in potash used in making explosives. After 1815 the kelp trade collapsed as Spanish barilla (*Salsola soda*) was once more available to the explosives manufacturers. The collapse of the kelp trade saw the effect of the Clearances bite much more deeply.

The Gaelic motto translated reads "Maintain our Right".

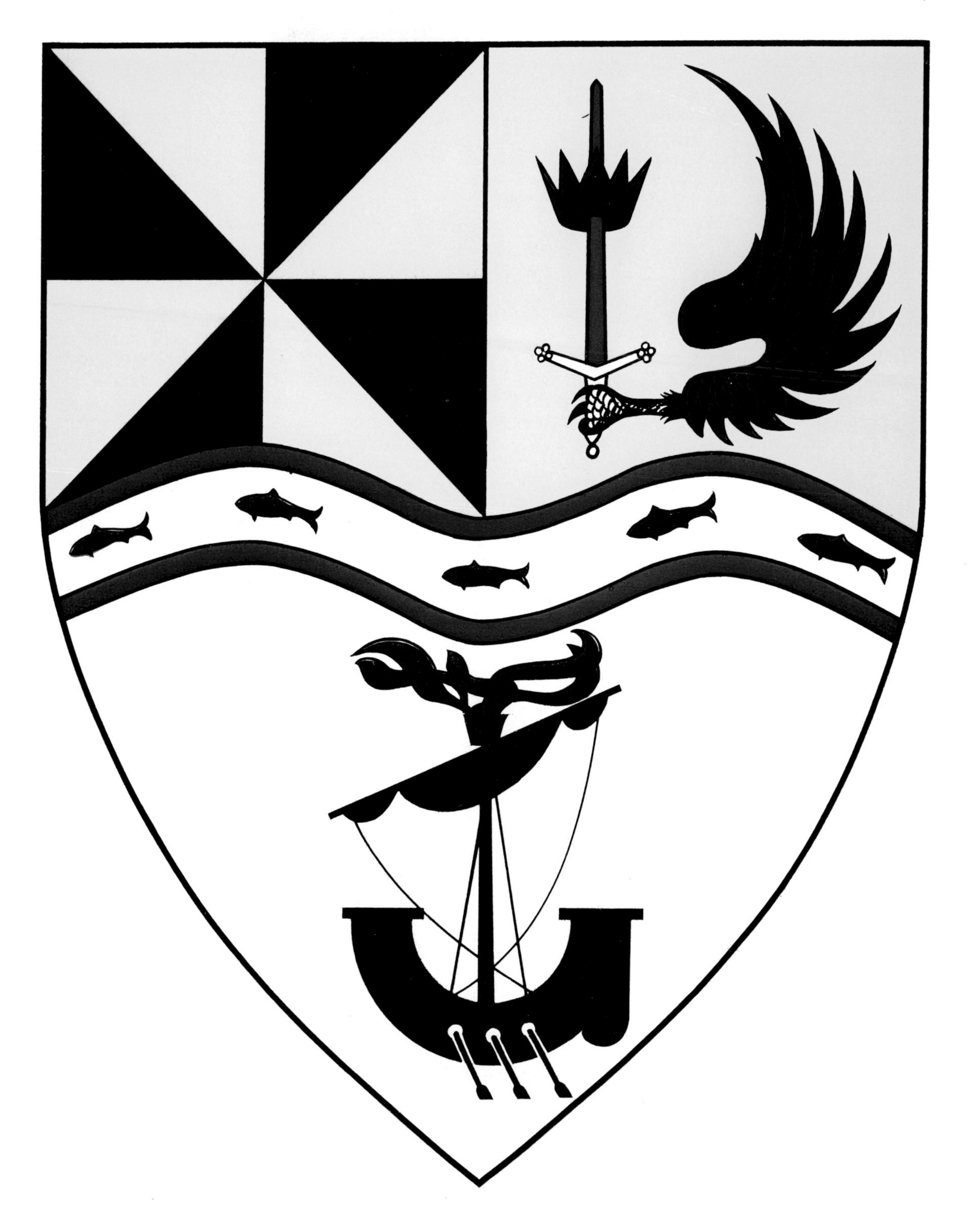

ARGYLL COUNTY COUNCIL

23. COUNTY COUNCIL OF THE COUNTY OF FIFE

"*Argent, a knight armed at all points on a horse at full speed, in his dexter hand a sword erect all Proper, his surcoat Argent, on his sinister arm a shield Or, charged with a lion rampant Gules, the visor of his helmet shut over which on a wreath of his liveries with a mantling of the fourth, doubled of the third, is set a lion rampant issuing out of the wreath, of the fourth, the caparisons of the horse of the last, fimbriated of the third, and thereon six shields of the last, each charged with a lion rampant of the fourth*".

MOTTO: "*Virtute et Opera*".

Of all the ancient Kingdoms that went to make up the Kingdom of the Scots, the one best remembered even until to-day is the Kingdom of Fife. The County Council arms show the Thane of Fife, armed, on his charger. The Earl's shield is of interest, being a red rampant lion on a field of gold. At one time the Earls of Fife, the MacDuffs, were the foremost Gaelic family in Scotland, and, indeed, it is a differenced form of the MacDuff arms that came to be worn by the Kings of Scots. The chief of the family of MacDuff had the hereditary duty of crowning the King of Scots. At the coronation of Bruce in 1306, Duncan, Earl of Fife, was opposed to Bruce, so Duncan's sister Isabel performed the ceremony and fulfilled the family obligation. This was an exceedingly courageous deed for Isabel, for not only was her brother fighting for Edward I of England, but so was her husband, and with a vengeance, for he was John Comyn, Earl of Buchan, kinsman to the Red Comyn murdered by Bruce before the altar of the Greyfriars in Dumfries just weeks before the coronation (8). Isobel MacDuff, wife of John Comyn, Earl of Buchan, paid the price for her bravery, and was caged in Berwick Castle for seven years, until released by Edward II of England. The last Earl of Fife of the original line, as Regent Albany, was first forfeited and then executed at Stirling Castle in 1425, by order of James I (14).

The Earls of Fife had an earlier form of arms than the red lion on its field of gold. This earlier form was "Paly Gules and Or"; that is vertical bars of red and gold. Within the territory of the Earls of Fife lived the Camerons of Ballegarno, and there is a theory that this family were the progenitors of the Camerons of Lochiel (19).

On a wild March night in 1286 on the cliffs south of Kinghorn, Alexander III was thrown from his horse and killed, and so ended the line of the Celtic Kings of Scots. Alexander II was married in Roxburgh Castle, and it was there that Alexander III was born in 1241. The latter was crowned at Scone, in 1249 following the death of his father on Kerrera. He married Margaret, a sister of Edward I of England, but she pre-deceased him and so did all their children. Alexander in an attempt to provide an heir married again in 1285 at Jedburgh, this time Yolande of Dreux, but there were no children — for the consequences of this see under the County Council of Berwick.

Not far from Kinghorn are two other places of note. Between Kinghorn and Inverkeithing lies Donibristle House, site of the murder of the Bonnie Earl o' Moray in 1592 (29). At Inverkeithing itself, in July 1651, Cromwell defeated a Scots force and advanced on Perth. This move by-passed the bulk of the Scots army lying at Stirling, and this army advanced into England where it met with disaster at the battle of Worcester in September 1651.

The County of Fife, along with its neighbouring county of Angus (formerly Forfar), was the home of a regiment of yeoman cavalry with a history going back to 1794. This formation — with the ancient Thane of Fife emblem as cap-badge — fought as two regiments Royal Armoured Corps in the 2nd World War, the regiments being named of course, The Fife and Forfar Yeomanry.

The motto "*Virtute et Opera*" ("By Virtue and Effort") is that of another MacDuff family to whom was granted the re-created Earldom in the mid-18th century.

FIFE COUNTY COUNCIL

24. COUNTY COUNCIL OF THE COUNTY OF ANGUS

"*Quarterly: 1st, Argent, a lion passant guardant gules, imperially crowned Or: 2nd, Gules, a cinquefoil Or; 3rd, Or, a fess chequy Azure and Argent, surmounted of a bend Gules, charged with three buckles of the field; 4th, Argent, a man's heart Gules, imperially crowned Or, on a chief Azure three mullets of the field*".

MOTTO: "*Lippin on Angus*".

In the arms of this County Council, attention is focused on four families who have held the Earldom of Angus — the Ogilvies, the Umfravilles, the Stewarts of Bonkyl, and the Red Douglases.

The first quarter displays the arms of the ancient Earldom of Angus, and this crowned lion, sometimes slightly differenced, forms the main charge on Ogilvie coats of arms. The second quarter displays the golden cinquefoil on its red ground of the senior line of the Umfraville family which became extinct with the death of Gilbert de Umfraville, in 1381. The third quarter bears the Stewart arms, differenced for Bonkyl, while the fourth quarter bears the Douglas arms differenced with the imperially crowned heart of the Bruce. The first Douglas to augment his arms with Bruce's heart was William, Lord of Douglas, son of the Good Sir James Douglas who was commissioned to take the Bruce's heart to the Holy Land, but who died in combat in Spain on the way (7). The further augmentation of the imperial crown was made to the arms of the Red Douglas in 1633 by the 11th Earl of Angus when he was created Marquis of Douglas (8).

Matilda, daughter and heiress of Malcolm, the last Celtic Earl of Angus (from whom the Ogilvy family are descended) conveyed the Earldom to her husband, John Comyn grandson of William Comyn, Earl of Buchan. John died and Matilda married again, this time Sir Gilbert de Umfraville, an Anglo-Norman baron, who in turn became Earl of Angus. Sir Gilbert was followed by three of his line: his own son Gilbert, a staunch follower of Edward I against the Scots; Gilbert's son Robert, a close adherent of Edward II and finally Gilbert, Robert's son — the last two were little if any more than nominally Earls of Angus, as the lands were taken by Robert the Bruce, who bestowed them on Sir John Stewart of Bonkyl, whose father, also Sir John Stewart, was killed fighting for Wallace (10, 11, 13, 14). The Earldom passed from the Stewarts to the Douglas family via Margaret Stewart, Countess of Angus and Mar, who bore a son to William, 1st Earl of Douglas (the Black Douglas). This son, George, became the first Douglas Earl of Angus and was also the progenitor of the Red Douglases.

Two of the royal burghs of Angus are particularly well known, Arbroath and Montrose. Arbroath has its ruined 15th century Abbey, founded by William the Lion in 1176. Not only is William the Lion buried here, but within the Abbey in 1320 Robert the Bruce set his seal to the Declaration of Arbroath, that ringing affirmation of Scotland's nationhood penned to convince Pope John XXII that the Scottish people would not stand for English interference — and convince Pope John it did. The other royal burgh whose name resounds through Scottish history is Montrose, the burgh named in the title of the chief of the Grahams, be he Earl, Marquis or Duke. The Graham lands lay largely on the lowland side of the highland line, yet the Graham leaders had a remarkable empathy with the highlanders — witness John Graham, Viscount Dundee, and James Graham, Marquis of Montrose. This singular empathy is seen again in 1782 when the then Marquis of Graham, later Duke of Montrose, saw to the repealing of the 1747 Act which had prohibited the wearing of tartan and highland dress.

The County Council's motto is a Scots form of "Trust in Angus".

ANGUS COUNTY COUNCIL

25. COUNTY COUNCIL OF THE COUNTY OF BANFF

"*Quarterly; 1st, Argent, a lion passant guardant Gules, crowned with an antique crown Or; 2nd, Argent two open crowns in fess Gules and a martlet in base Azure, on a chief of the last, a mullet of the field; 3rd, paly of six Or and Sable, on a fess Argent two roses Gules, barbed of the second and seeded of the first; 4th, Or, an open crown Gules, a chief chequy Azure and Argent; over all a pale engrailed per pale Vert and Sable voided Argent, charged with two chevronels Gules between three boars' heads erased Azure, armed Or and langued Sable*".

MOTTO: "*Spe et Spirtu*".

The most complex of the County Councils' arms are those of Banff, which allude to many aspects of the county's history. Basically the arms are quartered with a panel superimposed on the vertical division. This panel is engrailed, or toothed, down its sides, the right side as looked at being black, recalling the Sinclairs of Deskford whose black engrailed cross was marshalled in the arms of the Ogilvy Earls of Findlater and also of Seafield. While the Findlater line died out, the Seafield title was inherited by the chief of the Grants, who changed his surname from Grant to Ogilvy-Grant, and this is the surname of the present Earl of Seafield. The green edge on the left side, as looked at, is also engrailed, for symmetry. The chevronels and boar's heads on the panel recall the chevron and boars' heads of the Abercromby family. Lieutenant-General James Abercrombie, a British General in the Anglo-French "Seven Years War" in North America, won a place in history as the G.O.C. at the battle of Ticonderoga (1758), and his involvement in the subsequent ghostly tale centering round Major Duncan Campbell of Inverawe, of The Black Watch.

The first quarter shows the Ogilvy lion without its gorget, and wearing, instead of an imperial crown, an antique crown from the arms of Grant — the antique crowns of Grant may indeed hark back to an earlier family in the area, the Bissets. The second quarter is from the seal of the Cistercian Abbey of Kinloss, founded by David I in the 12th century. The Lordship of Balvenie is recalled by the red roses in the third quarter, the nominal rental of the Lordship to the Stewarts began as a red rose, "to be rendered if demanded" — inflation was not so troublesome then, for in 100 years this *reddendum* had risen to only three red roses, so one and a half roses on the arms of the County Council seems a fair compromise. The Lordship of Balvenie was first held by the Comyns (who built the castle) and after their fall from grace by the Black Douglases; on their fall the Lordship of Balvenie went to the Stewarts. The black and gold vertical bars are the arms of dominion of Atholl — the first Stewart Earl of Atholl was Walter son of Robert II and Euphemia of Ross (13, 21). Walter and his heir were executed for their involvement in the murder of James I at Perth in 1437. Sir John Stewart of Balvenie, son of Sir James Stewart, the Black Knight of Lorn (22), and of Joan Beaufort, widow of James I was created Earl of Atholl by James II c. 1457, and this started the long Stewart of Atholl connection with Balvenie, and hence the black and gold pales of Atholl in the arms of this county. Stewarts are also recalled in the fourth quarter, this time Stewart of Strathavon — the lower portion of whose arms are shown in this quarter (18). Alexander Stewart of Strathavon, illegitimate son of the Earl of Buchan, the "Wolf of Badenoch", by one means or another married Isobel Douglas, heiress and Countess of Mar (24). Isobel's first husband, Sir Malcolm Drummond, a brother of Queen Annabella, had been thrown into prison in 1402 on some pretext or other and kept there till he died, a process that took less than two years. Alexander Stewart of Strathavon presented himself at Kildrummy Castle in 1404, and by fair means or foul a union was effected between him and Isobel, Countess of Mar — thereafter Alexander Stewart styled himself Earl of Mar (18, 19). It was this Earl of Mar who suffered twice at the hands of Clan Donald, at Harlaw in 1411, and at Inverlochy in 1431.

The Latin motto is a good pun for the council responsible for the county bordered by the river Spey; in translation the motto reads "By Hope and Courage".

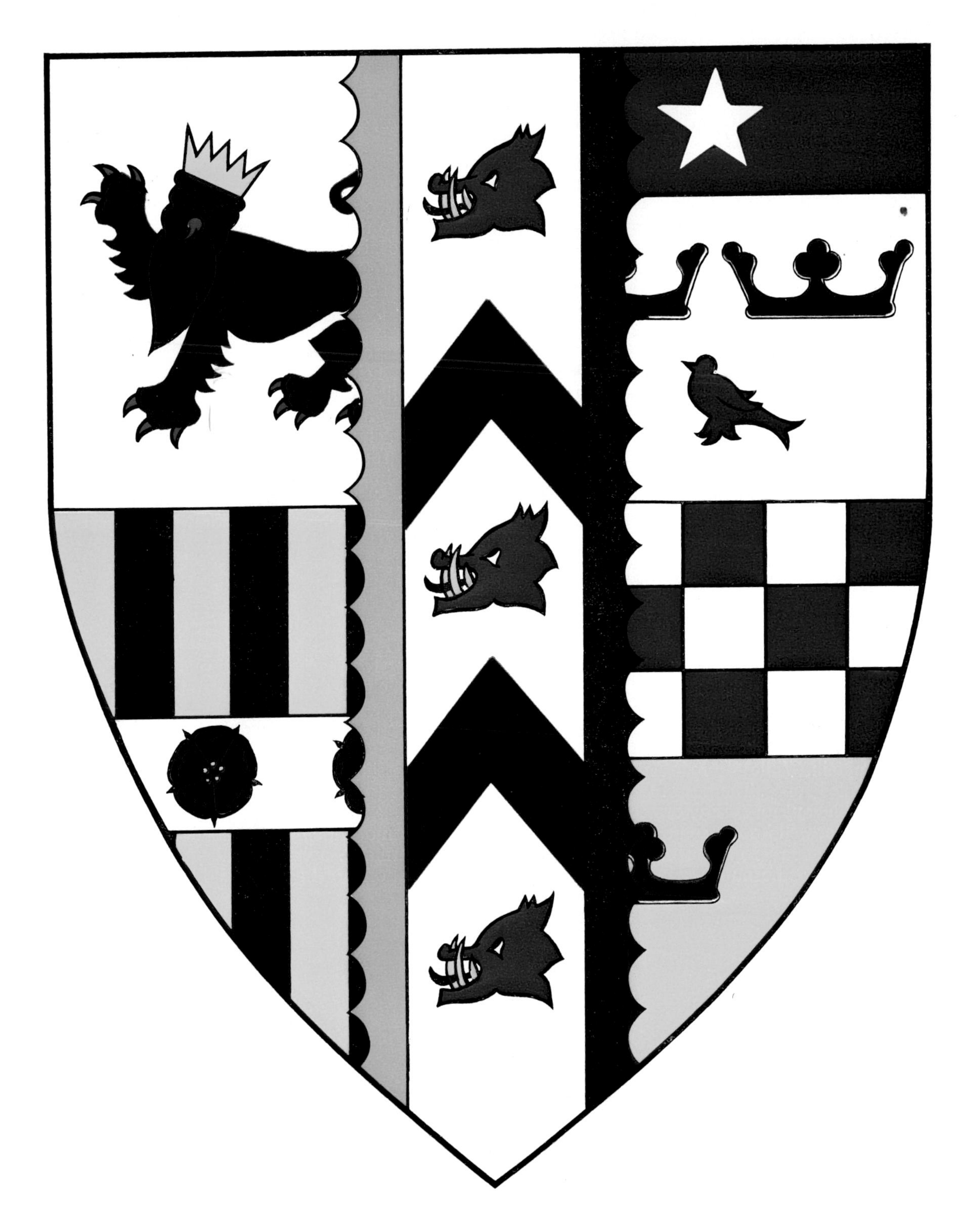

BANFF COUNTY COUNCIL

26. COUNTY COUNCIL OF THE STEWARTRY OF KIRKCUDBRIGHT

"*Azure, a lion rampant Argent, armed and langued Gules, crowned with an antique crown Or, surmounted by a bar chequy of the second and Vert*".

A large area of south-west Scotland anciently comprised the Lordship of Galloway. Because the Lords proved so powerful, the Lordship was whittled down to the size of the combined counties of Kirkcudbright and Wigtown, and hence the prominent place given to the Lion of Galloway in the arms of both County Councils. In the arms of the County Council of the Stewartry, the Lion of Galloway is differenced by having across it a checked bar. An heraldic bar is a diminutive of the fess, and in this case is from these stewards, the first being appointed by Archibald the Grim, that the county came to be known as "the Stewartry". It is said that the stewards used a green and white checked table-cloth as an aid to counting up the monies for which they were responsible.

The most famous daughter of the county is Devorgilla, heiress of Alan MacDowall, Lord of Galloway. Devorgilla married a Norman knight, Sir John Balliol of Barnard Castle, and this started a small chain reaction of historical events. Her husband, John Balliol, had had to provide lodgings and keep for sixteen poor students at Oxford, as recompense to the church for misdeeds he had committed in north-east England. When he died, his widow Devorgilla founded and endowed Balliol College, Oxford, in his memory. The arms of Balliol College to this day impale the arms of Balliol with the silver Lion of Galloway, though for some reason, here the Lion of Galloway is ducally crowned. Also in her husband's memory, Devorgilla founded and endowed Sweetheart Abbey near the Solway, where both she and her husband are buried, following Devorgilla's death at Barnard Castle in 1289. Devorgilla had a son, also called John, and this was the John Balliol who was for a short time King of Scots, from 1292 to 1294, and, during his disasterous reign, earned the nickname "Toom Tabard" or "Empty Coat" (3, 17).

In 1568, after the battle of Langside, Mary, Queen of Scots, fled to the county, to the Abbey of Dundrennan, founded by Fergus of Galloway. It was in May 1568 that Mary crossed the Solway and into England — the start of a tragic journey that had no ending for nearly eighteen years, till February 1587 at Fotheringay Castle, a castle ironically enough that had belonged once to Devorgilla of Galloway (13).

One famous son of the Stewartry was John Paul, who was born at Arbigland, Kirkbean, in 1747. Before he was a teenager he was an apprentice on a British merchantman — by the age of 21 John Paul was a Captain. While ashore in America after trans-Atlantic crossings he was befriended by an American family called Jones. The ties of friendship grew so strong that John Paul adopted the surname Jones, and as John Paul Jones is renowned as the founder of the U.S. Navy.

Another well-known son of the county was perchance born outside it. John Loudon MacAdam of tar-MacAdam fame gave a new word to the world in "tarmac". John MacAdam, of Lagwyne, Carsphairn, was born in Ayr in 1756 shortly after the family home of Lagwyne had been accidentally destroyed by fire.

STEWARTRY OF KIRKCUDBRIGHT

27. COUNTY COUNCIL OF THE COUNTY OF SUTHERLAND

"*Gules, on a fess Argent, between three mullets Or, a raven displayed Sable*".

MOTTO: "*Dluth lean do Dhutchas le Durachd*".

Sutherland is a name of Norse origin, *Sudrland*, meaning simply "South Land", Sutherland being the southernmost part of the Jarldom of Orkney. It is fitting that the arms of the County Council of Sutherland should bear such a strong Scandinavian imprint as that of the black raven of the Norse Jarls of Orkney, whose territory embraced the Counties of Caithness, Sutherland, and Shetland, in addition to Orkney itself.

On the retraction of Harold, Earl of Orkney, from the mainland of Scotland, William the Lion gave the "South Land" to Hugh of Moray, of the House of Freskin, a family of Flemish origin, and the same stock as the Murrays. The arms of Moray (2) are three silver stars on a blue field. Hugh of Moray, Lord of Sutherland, bore three gold stars on a red field and these arms formed the basis of the arms of the County Council. Hugh's son William was created Earl of Sutherland by Alexander II. The 2nd Earl, Kenneth, was killed at Halidon Hill in 1333 (3). The 8th and 9th Earls were none too fit, and in 1514 the 9th Earl was succeeded by his sister Elizabeth, wife of Adam Gordon, second son of the 2nd Earl of Huntly. Subsequent Earls of Sutherland until John the 16th Earl, bore the surname Gordon, and were in fact cadets of Huntly. The 16th Earl changed his name to Sutherland, but it was to stay that way for barely two generations, for Elizabeth, heiress of William, the 17th Earl married George Leveson-Gower.

At Carbisdale in the county, the Marquis of Montrose received his final defeat in April 1650. Still in the county, by Loch Assynt, he was captured and the long procession to Edinburgh started, ending the following month with the execution of Montrose. A narrative poem of that name by W. E. Aytoun commemorates this event.

The 93rd (Sutherland) Regiment, shortly to become known as the Sutherland Highlanders, was raised in 1800, on most feudal lines by Major-General William Wemyss of Wemyss, nephew of the late Earl of Sutherland. The Sutherland Regiment won great distinction in the Crimea by becoming the only foot regiment in the British Army with the battle honour "Balaclava". The 93rd became the 2nd Battalion, The Argyll and Sutherland Highlanders in 1881.

Mention "Sutherland" to a Scot, and his mind will likely go first, not to the Sutherland Regiment or to "Balaclava" (now more associated with "the Argylls"), but to the parishes of Farr and Lairg, and to Strathnaver, where in 1807 the most notorious and ruthless of the Highland Clearances started.

The Gaelic motto reads "Cling close to thy Heritage with Diligence" and perhaps recalls these clearances.

SUTHERLAND COUNTY COUNCIL

28. COUNTY COUNCIL OF THE COUNTY OF CAITHNESS

"*Azure, a galley Or, the sail thereof Argent, charged with a raven Sable*".

MOTTO: "*Commit thy work to God*".

Caithness occupies the extreme north-east mainland of Scotland: it was anciently occupied by Celts who were subdued and over-run by the Norsemen led by Sigurd, Jarl of Orkney. The Norse Jarls of Orkney held Caithness, nominally, as an earldom under the Scots crown. In 1196, William the Lion crossed the river Oykel and firmly annexed both Caithness and Sutherland. Caithness is now associated with the Norman-Scots house of Sinclair, and indeed the crest and motto used by the County Council is that of the Sinclair Earls of Caithness, The Sinclairs came by the Earldom of Caithness by marrying one of the co-heiresses of the Jarls of Orkney, the Lady Isobel, in the 13th century — the Jarldom of Orkney embraced also Caithness, Sutherland and Shetland. The son of this marriage, Henry Sinclair, became Jarl of Orkney, Norway's premier Jarldom under the Norwegian King Haakon VI (33). Not only was Henry Sinclair of Roslin, Midlothian, recognised in his claim to the Jarldom of Orkney by Haakon VI of Norway, but he was also Lord High Admiral of Scotland. As Norse influence receded to the Northern Isles of Scotland, the Sinclair mainland possessions were held without titled rank; this was amended when William, 3rd Sinclair Jarl of Orkney, was created Earl of Caithness by James II in 1455. James III required the 1st Earl of Caithness to relinquish his Norse rank; the 2nd Earl, also William, fell at Flodden in 1513 (3). It was the earlier William Sinclair who, in 1446, founded Roslin Chapel, Midlothian, with it's famed Prince's Pillar commemorating himself as Prince of Orkney. The Earldom of Caithness passed directly from this Earl William to George, the 6th Earl, with whom the line failed. George Sinclair was deeply in debt and he mortgaged his lands and titles to his major creditor, Sir John Campbell of Glenorchy. On the death in 1676 of this 6th Earl, John Campbell nipped in, married the widow, and assumed the title! Needless to say, a Sinclair was restored to the Earldom of Caithness, and as recompense, John Campbell of Glenorchy was created Earl of Breadalbane, in 1681.

With such a strong Norse element in the county's history, it is not surprising to see a Viking galley, or longship, in the County Council's arms. It is interesting to note that the Viking longship did not have a fighting-top, but a mast that could readily be stepped, and also that instead of a centrally mounted rudder, the longship had a *starbord* or steering oar mounted on what we now call the "starboard" side. The black raven shown on the sail was a powerful Norse battle emblem.

CAITHNESS COUNTY COUNCIL

29. COUNTY COUNCIL OF THE COUNTY OF MORAY

"*Quarterly; 1st and 4th, Azure, three mullets Argent: 2nd and 3rd, Argent, three cushions within a double tressure flory counterflory Gules*".

MOTTO: "*Sub Spe*".

Again one of Scotland's ancient Earldoms features strongly in the arms of one of her County Councils and this time it is the Earldom of Moray. Perhaps the first Earl of Moray known to most Scots is Thomas Randolph, kinsman and lieutenant of Bruce, renowned for "retrieving the rose from his chaplet" in turning back the troop of horse and killing their leader, Sir Robert Clifford of Skipton, on the eve of the battle of Bannockburn, 1314. If Clifford's party had won through to Stirling Castle there might not have been a Bannockburn for the Scots to have won. The next Earl of Moray to win a place in history was not so fortunate. This was James Stewart, Earl of Moray, half-brother of, and Regent for, Mary, Queen of Scots. Regent Moray was assasinated in January 1570 as he rode through Linlithgow, by James Hamilton of Bothwellhaugh. This James Stewart had a daughter Elizabeth, and she married another James Stewart, son of Sir James Stewart of Doune. Elizabeth's husband became Earl of Moray on his father-in-law's death. Luck was not with him either, for he too was murdered, though for different reasons. The reason given was Moray's alleged complicity in a treasonable raid led by Francis Stewart, Earl of Bothwell, on Holyrood in December 1591. The murder took place at the house of his mother, Lady Doune, at Donibristle in Fife in February 1592. The trigger to this murder was James VI's giving to George Gordon, Earl of Huntly, a commission to arrest Moray. There was no love lost between Huntly and Moray. and it is exceedingly doubtful if Huntly ever intended to arrest Moray. Huntly found it diplomatic to flee the country for a spell — but was made a Marquis on his return. The memory of this Earl of Moray is perpetuated in the haunting ballad, "The Bonnie Earl o' Moray".

Noo wae betide ye, Huntly
An' wharfore did ye sae?
I bad ye bring him wi' ye
But forbad ye him to tae slay.

Oh, lang may his lady look
Frae the Castle Doune
Ere she see the Earl o' Moray
Come soundin' through the toun.

In the County Council's arms the silver stars on their blue field are for the Earldom of Moray. This charge in different colours, is echoed through Scottish heraldry in perhaps all of the following families: Douglas, Murray, Sutherland and Innes. The red cushions surrounded by the royal augmentation, the red flory counterflory, are the arms of Bruce's lieutenant, Thomas Randolph.

Elgin, the county town, was the birthplace of two regiments still with us, though both in amalgamated form. At first sight it is remarkable that the two units, raised in consecutive years, should both be raised by MacKenzies and both be recruited from MacKenzie lands. The older of the two regiments—and indeed for long the second senior highland regiment—was raised in 1777 by Iain MacKenzie, Lord MacLeod, heir to the attainted Earl of Cromartie. This was the first regiment to channel the man-power of the Jacobite clans into the service of the Hanoverian Government. In 1808 this regiment's designation became the 71st, or Glasgow Highland Regiment — appropriately enough the Provost of Glasgow at that time was a MacKenzie. In 1881 the 71st and the 74th (Highland) Regiments were linked and came to be known as The Highland Light Infantry (City of Glasgow Regiment). Another amalgamation lay ahead, and in January 1959 the H.L.I. merged with the R.S.F. to become The Royal Highland Fusiliers (10).

In 1778 in Elgin, Kenneth MacKenzie, grandson of the attainted Earl of Seaforth, raised the unit known later as the 72nd Highland Regiment. The 72nd were linked with the 78th Highland Regiment in 1881 to form the Seaforth Highlanders. Again, another amalgamation lay ahead, for in 1961 the Seaforths and the Camerons (19) were amalgamated to form the Queen's Own Highlanders (Seaforth and Camerons).

It is interesting to note other points the H.L.I. and the Seaforths had in common. Both regiments wore the MacKenzie tartan (and their successors still do) a regimental march of each was "Blue Bonnets o'er the Border" — part of William Pitt's recruiting campaign? Another distinction the two regiments had in common, and this time a rare one, was that the 2nd Battalion of each regiment had an Assaye colour presented by the East India Company, which accounts for two of the three Assaye colours presented.

In English, the Latin motto reads "In Hope", and as in the arms of the County Council of Banff, puns on the river Spey.

MORAY COUNTY COUNCIL

30. COUNTY COUNCIL OF THE COUNTY OF ORKNEY

"*Parted per pale Azure and Gules: in the dexter a dragon galley Or, sails furled Argent, and in the sinister a lion rampant imperially crowned Or, armed and langued Azure, holding in its forepaws a battle-axe erect in pale Or*".

MOTTO: "*Boreas Domus Mare Amicus*".

The shield charges themselves could not be more Norse in origin. The left side as looked at is a Viking dragon-ship. A dragon-ship is thought to be a King's or Jarl's longship; the word viking is from the Norse *vik-ing*, meaning people of the inlet — Vik is not an uncommon place name in Norway to this day. The right side of the shield as looked at is singular indeed, being none other than the royal arms of Norway, differenced only by having the axe blade gold, and not silver. In Kirkwall, the building of St. Magnus' Cathedral was started in 1137 by Jarl Rognvald in memory of his uncle, who was joint Jarl of Orkney along with his cousin Haakon. The cousins Magnus and Haakon had totally different temperaments, Magnus being a "dove" while Haakon was a "hawk". Magnus was loved and respected in the Jarldom while Haakon was not — this so rankled with Haakon that on the island of Egilsay he treacherously slew Magnus. After Magnus' murder his saintliness was more fully appreciated and his body was exhumed from Egilsay and re-buried in the Cathedral in Kirkwall built in his honour. The builder of the Cathedral, Jarl Rognvald, was himself buried there in 1158.

In 1263 the Hebridean chiefs sought the aid of the King of Norway in their struggle against the King of the Scots. In answer to this plea Haakon IV of Norway sailed from Bergen with his battle-fleet in July, and headed down the west coast of Scotland and into the Firth of Clyde (12). In September he was beaten by the equinoctial gales at Largs, and with the remains of his fleet he limped northwards to Orkney where he died in his 60th year, before the end of 1263. Another member of the Norse royal house — and of the Celtic royal house — died in Orkney waters: Margaret, the Maid of Norway. Margaret was the grand-daughter of Alexander III (23) and she was Queen of Scots, albeit uncrowned, when she died in the arms of the Bishop of Bergen c. 1290 aged about 8 years. Margaret, Queen of Scots, is buried beside her mother in Bergen Cathedral.

Robert Stewart, a bastard of James V (the Guidman of Ballengeich), was granted the islands of Orkney and Shetland in 1564; in 1581 he was created Earl of Orkney. Earl Robert is less well-known than his son, Earl Patrick, who built for himself an unenviable reputation. It was Earl Partick who built Scalloway Castle, Shetland, c. 1600, and shortly afterwards the Earl's Palace at Kirkwall, c. 1607. Earl Patrick clashed with the Church over division of power in his Earldom, and was summoned to Edinburgh, imprisoned and executed in 1615, along with his son.

Events of national importance took place in Orkney in 1649 when the Royalist officer, William Hay, 3rd Earl of Kinnoul, landed from the continent with a small advance guard of Danish volunteers. In November of the same year one of the most important Royalist leaders, certainly for that particular time and place, died — Robert Douglas, 8th Earl of Morton and Lord of Orkney. Before the end of the year William Hay himself had died in Kirkwall. In March 1650 James Graham, 1st Marquis of Montrose landed in Orkney, at Kirkwall, and in early April Montrose, with his token force, crossed the Pentland Firth to Duncansby Head, to be defeated later in the month at Carbisdale (27). Not long afterwards Cromwell's soldiers were desecrating St. Magnus Cathedral.

The Latin motto reads "The North our Home the Sea our Friend", a very fitting motto for a County Council whose county was once part of a Norse Jarldom. Orkney County Council was only one of three of Scotland's County Councils to have supporters to their arms. Orkney along with Shetland became part of Scotland in 1468.

ORKNEY COUNTY COUNCIL

31. COUNTY COUNCIL OF THE COUNTY OF CLACKMANNAN

"*Or, a saltire Gules; a chief tierced per pale, in the 1st, Vert, a sinister gauntlet and in in the 3rd, (also Vert) a dexter gauntlet, both Proper, and in the 2nd, Argent, a pale Sable.*"

MOTTO: "*Look aboot Ye*".

Scotland's hero King, Bruce is remembered in the arms of Clackmannan County Council. The red saltire on its field of gold is from the arms of the Lordship of Annandale. Bruce's forbears, and indeed Bruce himself, was Lord of Annandale. Bruce's mother, Marjorie, was the heiress of Neil, the last Celtic Earl of Carrick, and both her husband and son became Earls of Carrick in her right, but there is no evidence that they used the arms of Carrick, (10) to any extent if at all — but they did use the arms of the Lordship of Annandale. Once this family of Norman origin came to Scotland as Lords of Annandale they ceased to use the family arms of Bruce, a blue lion rampant on a silver field, and instead used the arms of dominion of Annandale as their family arms. The English-based Bruces of Cleveland continued to use the original family coat of Bruce, but this family died out in the 13th century. Indeed, as King of Scots, Bruce wore as mantling for his helmet, cloth emblazoned with the Annandale arms. This latter usage can be seen illustrated in the 4½p postage stamp of the heraldic series of Britain, 1974. The present head of the Bruce family bears a differenced version of the Annandale arms, using as difference the family arms of Bruce.

In place of the red chief of the Annandale arms, the chief of this County Council's arms is divided into three equal parts. The outside parts bear a left and a right gauntlet. Legend has it that Bruce, on a visit to the Clackmannan area, left his gauntlet (*mannan*) on a stone (*clach*) and on discovering his loss, sent back his squire to look for the gauntlet, with the injunction, "Look aboot ye". The central division of the chief bears the arms of the Erskines, Earls of Mar and Kellie, whose seat is at Alloa, Clackmannanshire.

The Castle in Dollar Glen was originally a stronghold of the Stewarts of Innermeath, Lords of Lorn. The Lordship of Lorn passed to the Campbells of Lochawe by marriage. In 1457 Colin Campbell was created 1st Earl of Argyll, and it was probably he who built the tower known as "The Gloume". This 1st Earl of Argyll proved so helpful to the crown that James IV decreed in 1490 that the name of the castle be changed from Castle Gloom to Castle Campbell. It was this same Colin Campbell who around 1484 imprisoned his infant grandson — who just happened to be the grandson also of John II of Islay, Lord of the Isles. This grandson of both was the infant Donald *Dubh*, and his prison, Innis Chonnel in Loch Awe, opposite Dalavich. Young Donald *Dubh* — he is not the onc of the pibroch (19) —had been abducted by John Stewart of Balvenie, Earl of Atholl (25) and hence the Stewart of Atholl motto, "Furth fortune and fill the fetters". It was not long till John Stewart and his Countess were in fetters — in Claig Castle on Fraoch Eilean off Jura. Archibald Campbell , 8th Earl and 1st Marquis of Argyll, and James Graham 5th Earl and 1st Marquis of Montrose, were on opposite sides in the internecine strife of 17th century Scotland. Montrose tried to take Castle Campbell in 1645, but it proved too big a task for him. The Castle was taken in 1654 by General Monck, founder of the Coldstream Guards (3). In nearby Menstrie, nestling below Dumyat in the Ochils, is the 16th century fortified house of the Alexanders. "Alexander" is but an anglicised form of the Kintyre surname "MacAlister", an early branch of Clan Donald. In 1567 Sir William Alexander was born here, later becoming 1st Earl of Stirling, the man behind the money-making idea of the Nova Scotia baronetcies.

CLACKMANNAN COUNTY COUNCIL

32. COUNTY COUNCIL OF THE COUNTY OF KINROSS

"*Argent, on an island Proper, in a loch undy Azure and of the field, a castle also Proper*".

MOTTO: "*For all Time*".

Loch Leven Castle wholly occupies and completely dominates the arms of Kinross County Council as indeed the island fortress must at one time have all but overwhelmed the minds of its many captives. Loch Leven Castle must have been looked upon as one of Scotland's major prisons, for the prisoners consigned to it were of high degree: for example, Alexander Stewart, Earl of Buchan, better known as the "Wolf of Badenoch"; in 1369 Robert II, two years before he came to the throne; in 1431 Archibald, 5th Earl of Douglas ("Bell the Cat") (3), and by far the most famous, in 1567 Mary, Queen of Scots. Mary was imprisoned here after the "non-event" of Carberry Hill near Pinkie in Midlothian, when she surrendered to the Lords of the Congregation after bidding farewell to her third husband, James Hepburn, 4th Earl of Bothwell, whose subsequent journeyings were to end with a madman's death in a Danish dungeon. It was while captive in Loch Leven Castle that Mary, on 24th July 1567, was forced to abdicate in favour of her son by Henry Stewart, Lord Darnley. Her one-year old son was crowned James VI in Stirling just five days later, with Mary's half-brother James Stewart, Earl of Moray as Regent (11, 15, 17). Incidentally, the Earl of Moray was also the half-brother of William Douglas of Loch Leven, Keeper of Loch Leven Castle. Men were very prudent in these days, and it was stated at the outset that, failing the Earl of Moray, James Douglas 4th Earl of Morton should be Regent — and indeed just over a year and a half after the assassination of Moray, Morton became Regent. Morton was Regent for barely six years, resigning in March 1578. By 1580 he was openly accused of complicity in Darnley's murder, brought to trial and executed in July 1581 (6, 12). On the execution of James Douglas, Earl of Morton, the title passed to — William Douglas of Loch Leven.

Mary was more fortunate — for a time anyway. With the help of young Willie Douglas, she made her escape. The castle was locked once she was outside, and the castle keys dropped in the Loch as Willie Douglas rowed his Queen to freedom. Mary was met on the shore by a small party led by George, 5th Lord Seton — brother of one of "the Queen's Four Marys" — and the small cavalcade headed for the Seton stronghold of Niddrie Castle in West Lothian. From Niddrie Castle Mary made for Dumbarton Castle, prior to the battle of Langside.

Burleigh Castle, near Loch Leven, dates from early in the 16th century and was the home of the Balfours of Burleigh. The eldest son of Sir James Balfour of Pittendreich became Lord Balfour of Burleigh in 1606. Sir James Balfour — an eminent lawyer, and one-time galley slave — is thought to have been involved in two notable murders. The first, that of Cardinal Beaton in May 1546, and the second that of Henry Stewart, Lord Darnley, second husband of Mary, Queen of Scots, who was the elder son of Matthew, 4th Earl of Lennox, and of Margaret Douglas (daughter of Archibald, 6th Earl of Angus, and Margaret Tudor), at Kirk o' Field, Edinburgh 1567.

When the motto was chosen, the County Councillors had not reckoned with the Local Government (Scotland) Act of 1974.

KINROSS COUNTY COUNCIL

33. COUNTY COUNCIL OF THE COUNCIL OF ZETLAND

"*Azure, a base invected barry Argent and Sable, the alternate party lines being engrailed and plain, a dragonship oars in action Or, under sail spread to starboard Argent, flag and mast Gules*".

MOTTO: "*Med Lögum Skal Land Byggja*".

Firstly, Zetland or Shetland? 'Shetland' is the spelling normally used. The name is thought to be derived from the Norse *hjaltland* meaning high land, though other meanings are given. Over the centuries the name has been spelt with an initial 'H' then 'Y', and finally 'S'. There was a period when 'Z' was confused with 'Y' and it is from the 'Z' confusion that we get the spelling 'Zetland'. Native Shetlanders do not subscribe to the 'Zetland' spelling, but, paradoxically, this was the legally accepted form, and hence that used by the County Council.

Shetland was part of the Norse Jarldom of Orkney, and, together with Orkney, retained its intimate connection with Scandinavia long after the remainder of the Jarldom, Caithness and Sutherland, had been absorbed into Scotland; Shetland is just over 200 sea miles from Bergen, but is more like 350 miles from Edinburgh by sea. It is interesting to note, however, that only the first three Jarls were of pure Norse blood before it became diluted with Celtic and Norman blood — maybe "dilution" is the wrong word to use regarding the introduction of Norman blood, for this could be regarded as partly a back-cross!

Shetland along with Orkney was grudgingly given by King Christian I of Norway, Sweden and Denmark as the dowry on the marriage of his only daughter, Margaret, to James III; the treaty of acquisition was ratified by Christian in 1468. The dowry was to be sixty thousand florins, but when King Christian had to admit that his treasury did not contain anything like this sum, it was agreed that Orkney and Shetland should be given in lieu, first as a pledge and then completely.

The dragon-ship on the shield is the type of longship attributed to a Viking chief, who in this case could be the Jarl of Orkney, whose territory embraced Shetland. The Scottish successors to the Jarls of Orkney were the Sinclair Earls of Caithness, and it is because of this Sinclair link that the sea on the arms of Zetland County Council is black engrailed silver, reminiscent of the black engrailed cross of the Sinclair arms.

In mid-16th century, the royal estates of Orkney and Shetland were "in hand", but in 1564 Mary, Queen of Scots, granted the Northern Isles to her younger half-brother, Robert Stewart. In 1581 James VI created Robert Earl of Orkney; both Earl Robert and his successor, Earl Patrick Stewart, were notorious for their cruelty and misgovernment. It was Earl Patrick who built Scalloway Castle around 1600, as his Shetland base, though his principal seat was at the Earl's Palace, in Kirkwall Orkney. Earl Patrick's misdeeds caught up with him when he and his son were executed in Edinburgh in 1615, primarily for trying to gain more power in his Earldom at the expense of the Church.

The motto in old Norse, is from the *Njalssaga* (Njal's Saga) and means "By law is the land established".

ZETLAND COUNTY COUNCIL

REFERENCES

The following publications have been found most helpful;

"A History of the House of Douglas" *(2 Volumes)*
by Sir Herbert Maxwell
published by Freemantle, 1902.

"Ordinance Gazetteer of Scotland" *(3 Volumes)*
by Francis H. Groome
published by Thomas C. Jack, 1886.

"The Clans, Septs & Regiments of the Scottish Highlands"
by Frank Adam and Innes of Learney
published by W. & A. K. Johnston, 1952.

"Tartans of the Clans & Families of Scotland"
by Sir Thomas Innes of Learney
published by W. & A. K. Johnston, 1945.

"Scots Heraldry"
by Sir Thomas Innes of Learney
published by Oliver & Boyd, 1956.

"The Highlands "
by Calum I. MacLean
published by Batsford, 1959.

"The Camerons: A History of Clan Cameron"
by John Stewart of Ardvorlich
published by The Clan Cameron Association, 1974.

"Burke's Encyclopaedia of Heraldry"
by John Burke and John Bernard Burke
published by Henry G. Bohn, 1844.

"The Illustrated Gaelic — English Dictionary"
by Edward Dwelly
published by Gairm Publications, 1973.

To any readers whose interest in Scots heraldry has been aroused, the following publications will prove indespensible:

"SIMPLE HERALDRY"
by Iain Moncreiffe & Don Pottinger
published by Thomas Nelson, Edinburgh.

The map "SCOTLAND OF OLD"
by Iain Moncreiffe & Don Pottinger
published by John Bartholomew & Son, Edinburgh.

In addition I should like to accord my very sincere thanks to two authors who set me off on the Scottish history trail quite a long time ago. H. E. Marshall, author of "Scotland's Story — A history of Scotland for boys and girls" and Dorothea K. Broster, authoress of "The Flight of the Heron", "The Gleam in the North", "The Dark Mile" and"Almond, Wild Almond".